D1605968

Growing Up Observed: Tales from Analysts' Children

Growing Up Observed: Tales from Analysts' Children

Edited by
Herbert S. Strean

The Haworth Press
New York • London

Growing Up Observed: Tales from Analysts' Children was also published as *Current Issues in Psychoanalytic Practice,* Volume 4, Numbers 1/2, Spring/Summer 1987.

The Haworth Press, Inc., 12 West 32 Street, New York, NY 10001
EUROSPAN/Haworth, 3 Henrietta Street, London WC2E 8LU England

Library of Congress Cataloging-in-Publication Data

Growing up observed.

Published also as Current issues in psychoanalytic practice, v. 4, nos. 1/2.
Includes bibliographical references.
1. Psychoanalysts — Family relationships — Case studies. 2. Parent and child — Case studies. I. Strean, Herbert S.
RC506.G778   1987   150.19'5'0922   87-21080
ISBN 0-86656-634-1

Growing Up Observed: Tales from Analysts' Children

Current Issues in Psychoanalytic Practice
Volume 4, Numbers 1/2

CONTENTS

Growing Up Observed: Tales from Analysts' Children

LETTER FROM THE EDITOR

Dear Reader,

How do psychoanalysts' children feel about their parents? How emotionally healthy are the offspring of analysts? Are they more mature than children of parents from other professional persuasions? What are their unique difficulties? What are their unique strengths?

These questions and other ones about the children of analysts are frequently asked, but are rarely answered to our satisfaction. Little research has been done on the subject, yet the dynamics of the analyst's child continues to arouse a great deal of curiosity.

This issue is an attempt to learn more about how analysts' children feel toward their "analyst-parent," how they feel about themselves and how they relate to those around them. We recognized from the beginning of this undertaking that our sample is a skewed one—we heard only from those analysts' children who felt safe enough and interested enough to share their perceptions, their concerns, their loves and their hates, with our readers. How representative our sample, is something about which we cannot be sure. Yet, our writers, who range from seven years old to over eighty, provide some clues as to how analysts' children relate to their own parents and to their own worlds.

Like all children, our sample of writers consistently express considerable ambivalence toward their parents. Analysts' children seem to appreciate their parents for their understanding but also resent them for it. Analysts, according to their children, talk too much in the language of "psychoanalese" and do not react enough with sufficient emotional spontaneity. Analysts, according to our writers, work too many hours, and are not physically and emotionally available enough to their children. Perhaps other themes will emerge in your mind as you read the essays of our writers.

In addition to papers from analysts' children we have interesting articles on "The Analyst as Parent" by Polly Condit and "The Careers of Children of Psychoanalysts" by Richard Friedman. We have also republished a paper on "Psychotherapy With Children of Psychotherapists" which I wrote almost twenty years ago.

We are indebted to our friend and colleague, Mrs. Edith Elson for the provocative title of this issue, "Growing Up Observed."

We trust that this issue will be of interest to you. If so, let us know. Maybe we should hear from the spouses of analysts, the parents of analysts, etc.?

Cordially,
Herbert S. Strean
Editor

PART I

Life with Father:
Franz Alexander, MD

Francesca Alexander, PhD

Lucy Freeman, associate editor of this journal, and I had frequently discussed the possibility of my working on an autobiographical work in which my life with my father would be featured. This project always stayed in the somewhat nebulous state of, "Gee, that's a great idea and I'll get to it sometime in the future." But on January 22, 1986 Lucy wrote me a note once more discussing this project. I looked at the date, and decided now was the time. It's not that it is really a more convenient time, but January 22 was my father's birthday.

Looking back on the period of growing up, and adulthood I realize that my views concerning both my parents have obviously undergone several radical changes. Moving from resentment to admiration, and finally to compassion has taken me a long time. But, above all, it is still difficult for me to realize there was something different or special in growing up as the daughter of one of the pioneers of psychoanalysis. It's difficult to recognize this was a unique situation because when you are growing up in a given family there is little to measure it against and see how it compares with the way other people grow up.

Francesca Alexander is with the Department of Sociology, California State University, Los Angeles.

3

WHAT WAS HE LIKE?

First of all my father, like all fathers, had a definite personality, relationship with his wife, and children. Like anyone else when he was home, he was not playing the role of Franz Alexander, director of one of the first Institutes for Psychoanalysis in this country, but was a man with his own hopes, fears, and passions. He didn't share these private aspects of himself with many, in fact, he was a private man. It was only during the last few years of his life, and the intervening years, that I have been able to know him. And in the past two years, some twenty years after his death, I've gotten to know him even better, or at least differently. This has been made possible because I've had the opportunity to obtain personal papers, letters, films, and tapes that my parents kept over the years—many dating back to times before I was born. The Institute for Psychoanalysis in Chicago established the Alexander archives, and I felt that these documents belonged there. I gathered them together, studied them, and sent them "home" to the Institute. For me this has become a period of learning, and growth. It has helped fulfill a gap in my own understanding, and also made it possible to provide a living legacy for others, not the least of whom is my son, Alexander Levine.

My father was a man who was hesitant about being close with others, and at the same time needed the sustained support of others around him. He was courageous and needful; he was forward looking and clung tenaciously to tradition. These contradictions marked many people who had frequent interactions with him.

As I look back, I realize that my father had a hard time dealing with his children. He really wasn't comfortable with us. Often his behavior was stiff, or abstracted. At the time, I felt he didn't really care about me and my sister. I remember when I was in first grade he came up to me and asked, "What did you learn in school today?" I was delighted to have his interest and attention. I poured out the activities and adventures of the day. He made some noncommittal comment and went on with his work at his desk. Later that evening after dinner, he once more looked at me when I was walking through the living room, and asked, "What did you do in school today?" I was angry, and hurt. He hadn't remembered. I responded by saying, "You don't care."

The episode was repeated many times throughout my school years. As time went by my responses became more angry, but the feeling of being depreciated also continued. My mother would often point out the obvious by saying, "It doesn't matter what you tell him, he won't remember anyway." Her bitterness probably stemmed from the same root, she too wanted more attention than she received. My father had a love affair with work. As I look back, it seems that he must have been molded by a Puritan culture which demanded that he produce. Rare was the day even on vacations or weekends that he did not spend several hours at home at his desk writing or making notes on something. None of this is supposed to mean that he didn't play with us. I remember many Sundays in the winter when my father would take me ice-skating at the Lincoln Park lagoons. It was during those days I developed a habit I still have of avidly reading the weather forecasts in the paper. I didn't look forward to the Spring thaw. The summers were O.K. too when we were in our summer home in La Jolla, California; in La Jolla he would play tennis with me.

HOW DO YOU LIVE WITH PSYCHOANALYSIS?

As a child, I didn't know what psychoanalysis was, nor the prominent position my father held in what was at that time a slightly deviant occupation. I do remember that if I told my school friends that my father was a psychoanalyst they would often express puzzlement. "What's that?" It was hard to explain, and when I did I often felt that being a doctor who cured crazy people didn't really gain their admiration. After a few years of this, I learned to answer the question, "What does your father do?" with the simple response, "He's a doctor." Somehow this had more credibility and status than being a psychoanalyst.

At home my father would also talk about the difficulty of convincing the established medical men to recognize the value of psychoanalysis. Often at dinner he would discuss with my mother the fact that many of Chicago's medical community seemed to feel that if you couldn't find an organic cause for some aberrant behavior then you didn't have a legitimate illness. How pleased he was when some internists, allergists, and even surgeons recognized the validity of psychodynamic explanations of human behavior. I often thought that one of the reasons he got involved in psychosomatic medicine was to create a path of common interest with those who practiced traditional medicine, as well as an intellectual concern with the field. I remember asking him why only physicians should be trained as psychoanalysts. His explanation was simple. When we came to this country and helped bring psychoanalysis here, he believed psychoanalysis still didn't have much credibility, but physicians did. He said, ''If doctors with their status practice this specialty, then it will more quickly receive acceptance by Americans.'' The truth of his contention that the medical community did not accept this new area as legitimate can be seen in the year he spent as professor of psychoanalysis at the University of Chicago which ended in near disaster. He was not understood by the medical community; the medical school faculty shunned his lectures, although the social and behavioral sciences supported him.

As I look back on it now, there were a few special problems in being the daughter of a psychoanalyst. First of all, just like the child of a minister, my sister and I were often regarded as being different, and of being expected to be ''normal.'' How I learned to hate the word ''normal.'' The questions I asked myself, reflections of the questions that had been asked of me by my parents and others, focused my thoughts on examining my actions, thoughts and feelings for their normalcy. Later, virtual strangers would come up to me and ask, ''Does your father psychoanalyze you?'' I always felt embarrassed by these questions; they reflected the ignorance of the person doing the questioning, and alluded to the perennial question about being normal.

When I was approaching my fifth birthday, my father asked one morning if I had dreamt the night before. I said, ''Yes.'' He responded, ''What did you dream about?'' I told him with enthusiasm that I had dreamt about getting a toy car for my birthday—the kind you can sit in and pedal to make it go. When asked what I wanted for my birthday, I told both my parents I wanted a large teddy bear that I had seen in a department store. When my birthday came around, I got the toy car. It was pretty, a taxi-cab type, complete with passenger seat, and trunk loaded with tools. But, it was not what I wanted. My father misinterpreted my dream. Years later when I was in analysis, I discovered that cars have always been a frequent symbol in my dreams, but they rarely, if ever, have any relationship to means of transportation. At any rate, I quickly learned to keep my dreams to myself. Other events in life with which most people cope without undue stress, became major in my family. For example, when I had my first menstrual period I had known what to expect since my mother had explained sexual maturation to me, and I felt fine about "growing up." However, that night when my father came home, I overheard my mother tell him that I had "become a woman." His immediate response was, "Do you think she'll need to be analyzed?" Once again, I was forced to examine my reactions to my maturity and see if they were "normal."

Later in my adolescence when I desperately felt the need to get some psychotherapy, it wasn't so easy. Then I had to convince my father not of my normalcy, but of my desperation. At the end of high school, I went into a depression. I could not find direction or meaning in my life. I explained to my parents that I was miserable; they didn't want to believe me until I threatened suicide. That got attention, and help. The problem then became who should analyze Alexander's daughter. It had to be a colleague who liked and respected him, but who also would not be intimidated by him. The search ended when a member of the Institute, but not one of the established faculty, was chosen. The choice was good, and in a few years I graduated to my second analyst, a training analyst but again not one of the Institute's faculty. It was only years later that I realized this was not only a painful period for me, but it must have also been difficult for my father. After all one of his children needed professional help; somewhere something in my formative years had gone wrong or had been neglected.

Sometimes I think psychoanalytic theory jeopardized my growing up. As most children, I wanted to be close to my parents. However, my father always kept me at arms length. The shades of Oedipus were so strong that when I came home on a vacation after graduating college my father shook hands with me, but avoided putting his arms around me. I think I had worked through my feelings, but had he ever addressed his own?

FAMILY RELATIONSHIPS

As in every family, each person played a particular role vis à vis the other members. My father was central in the family in as much as his schedule and his needs were always considered first, and family life revolved around that schedule. He was not central in that he was so frequently absent, or involved in his work that a great deal of actual living was done without his presence. My mother was the dominant figure in the house because she organized everything, and was present. She played a peculiar role in relation to my father in that she was his constant support, and confidant, yet she also felt she was the one to make sure that he did not develop an overwhelming sense of self-importance. Mother liked to tell him and us the truth, especially if the truth could be somewhat negative or critical. I feel that mother also believed the primary responsibility for raising both my sister and myself was hers. She was the one who showed concern about our well-being.

My sister, who looks a lot like my mother, was my father's daughter. By that I mean she was not expected to be a career woman, or to make a name for herself. She was decorative, and raised to play the traditional role of woman. I, the younger, did not have such a straightforward definition of my destiny. When I was born both my parents were hoping to have a son. Inadequate though I was to play that role, that was the one I was cast into. I remember both my parents would say to me, "You must have a career, that is something no one can take away from you and you need not depend on anyone else then." I guess I never really thought of not having a career; the big problem was to choose what I should do. From the time I entered high school, my father repeatedly asked me to go into medicine, and then assured me I could become the next director of the Institute. As I gained knowledge about the larger world, I questioned whether or not the Institute should or would tolerate a family dynastic rule. He brushed these considerations aside. However, I did not want to become another psychoanalyst; I found that I needed an identity larger than, and more personal than, being Dr. Alexander's daughter. When I was a little girl, Anna Freud was often held up to me by my mother as representing the dangers of not developing one's own identity: "If you don't work on being somebody yourself, you can be like Anna Freud, who is important only because she stands in the shadow of her father." Although I believe my mother's assessment of Anna Freud is wrong, it still explains my effort at developing my own direction in life. When I met people during my years in college and later, I was often asked "Aren't you Alexander's daughter?" When I answered yes, I frequently wanted to add, "but I'm somebody too." Perhaps to escape this identification, I first majored in English at college. What could be a farther cry from psychoanalysis? Later, however, I decided that I needed something more alive than dusty tomes, and earned my doctorate in sociology. Interestingly enough, I don't think I was consciously aware that much of my father's interest was in sociology, which can be seen in at least two of his books—*Our Age of Unreason* and *The Western Mind in Transition*.

WHO WERE THEY?

Who were my parents? My father was the first son of a Hungarian professor of philosophy. Evidently his gender played an extremely important role in his family because both of his parents had looked forward to producing a son after having had three daughters. His father was prominent in the intellectual circles of Budapest, and urged his son to follow a somewhat similar career. Despite this urging, my father elected to study medicine, an occupation not defined as an intellectually acceptable career in pre-World War I Europe. He graduated from medical school just in time to become a physician in the Austro-Hungarian army. The first two years of the war, he was medical officer on a hospital train traveling from Vienna to Budapest. They were years of adventure for him; he always spoke with fondness of this period. It was his first time away from home, and he had a position of respect and authority. The second two years of the war were not so easy. He was assigned to be a medical officer on the Italian front. It was during this period that he met my mother. She was a novitiate in a convent in the Alps of northern Italy. The convent had been evacuated because the Austro-Hungarian troops were invading, but mother was left behind, sick with typhoid fever and malaria. When my father chose the convent's buildings to be the field hospital, she was there. He administered medical care; she survived and eventually married him.

She was not brought up to be married. Her mother had placed her in the convent when she was a school girl. Her mother had, in keeping with medieval tradition, "given her to the church." A daughter of a titled family whose father had been killed in a duel prior to her birth, she had been raised to be a nun. After my mother and father married, they were separated by the war's end. With the armistice declared, my father returned to Budapest to be demobilized. It was a period of political unrest and revolution. It became virtually impossible for him to communicate with his new wife, who had remained in Italy. Through the good efforts of his parents and younger brother, who had all fled to Switzerland, the young couple were reunited in Berlin. During this chaotic post-war period in Germany, characterized by a frightening run-away inflation, mother became pregnant. Despite this, she earned money by writing movie subtitles for foreign films. This was my parents' primary source of income during which time my father studied to become a psychoanalyst. He entered the Berlin Institute in 1920; he was the first candidate at the world's first formal psychoanalytic training institute. Evidently, aside from his new interest in psychoanalysis, his other main interest was survival. Frequently, he wrote various family members begging to borrow money, selling his furniture and buying it back. Despite the hardship, my sister was born and the family prospered. Some six years later, I was born. My father began to achieve recognition, even from Freud, who encouraged him to continue his writing and thinking on various theoretical psychoanalytic issues.

In 1929, Robert Hutchins, president of the University of Chicago, met my father at an International Psychoanalytic Congress. He offered him an appointment as a professor of psychiatry at the University of Chicago. My father rejected this offer, insisting that Hutchins change the appointment to visiting professor of psychoanalysis. When this was agreed on, my father left for Chicago; mother, my sister, and I followed some months later. It took courage for my father to go to the United States since he had already established an enviable professional record in Berlin. Freud and others warned him about the pitfalls of America. Freud explained that he considered America to be partly barbaric, and crassly materialistic, where science would be impeded by the American tendency to solve all problems with money. It was only a year ago when I had the opportunity to read twenty-two unpublished letters from Freud to my father that I realized the depths of Freud's distrust of American culture. Despite these warnings, we moved West to America.

After a difficult year in Chicago, we went to Boston where my father worked with William Healy of the Judge Baker Foundation. Life was always dramatic. While we were in Boston, mother received a note telling her that my sister and I would be abducted if she did not pay a certain preventive ransom. It was during the days of the Lindberg kidnapping, and mother demonstrated her distrust and fear by simply taking my sister and myself to New York without leaving word with anyone. Once in New York, she phoned my father to explain what happened. After several weeks, when she felt things were safe again, we returned to Boston. I have no idea how my father got along during this period of unplanned trauma. While we were in Boston, he was asked by members of the Julius Rosenwald Foundation if he would be willing to set up an Institute for Psychoanalysis patterned after the one in Berlin. My father agreed on condition that the Institute would be in Chicago where he had already met the distrust of the medical community. He was determined to change their perception of this new specialty. It took several years, but he did achieve his goal. During his tenure the Institute played an important role in determining who received medical residencies in psychiatry in Chicago teaching hospitals.

FAMILY LIFE

In some ways, we were definitely an atypical family. One of the things that characterized us was a family tradition that all hostile feelings were to be openly, verbally expressed. We learned early that such feelings were not considered bad or good but that they were there and would not be denied. This allowed a more open interaction among us than was customary during the 1930s in upper middle-class America. I wasn't aware of this difference until I invited friends to my home and they were clearly astonished when I told one of my parents to "drop dead." My friends exclaimed, "How can you talk that way?" I was puzzled; what had I done wrong? It took some time for me to learn that what was acceptable at home had to be curbed in company. Looking back on it now, I realize that some feelings were not given expression. Essentially, we did not refer to our feelings of inadequacy, longing, and uncertainty. It was only years later that I learned my father was very concerned about his place in the community, and was even more anxious about his move to California when he retired from the Institute. His apprehension centered on whether or not he would find acceptance by his peers on the West Coast, where he was not even licensed to practice. His concerns were expressed to my mother, but to no one else.

We entertained a great deal, or at least so I thought. Frequently, we had other psychoanalysts over to our house, and a fair collection of social scientists from the University of Chicago. Again, I didn't realize at the time what an intellectually rich field I was growing up in. What I did realize was that we had company again, and that immediately after dinner I would be excused to go to my room while mother was busy entertaining the wives of the guests, and my father and the men would go to his study and discuss current issues. Few of these discussions took place in the open since psychoanalytic thinking was not really open at that time. Some of those guests stand out in my memory. It was Karl Menninger who noticed that our apartment, richly equipped with books, did not contain any reading material for me. Two days later, after he had returned to Topeka, he sent me a copy of *Bambi*. For many years thereafter, I could count on books from Karl Menninger.

Shortly after the Institute's birth, we spent a summer vacationing in California, driving from North to South along the coast. When we arrived in La Jolla, we stayed a few weeks. Mother was taken with the place. On the train returning to Chicago, mother announced to all of us she had bought two lots on the ocean front in La Jolla, and was scheduled to return there in November to begin building a house. My father was the most surprised of all at my mother's independent action. The questions regarding why, how, and what arrangements she would make for our care when she went back to the West Coast were many. She assured us we would be provided for by our household help, and that she would return in time for Christmas. That winter saw a great deal of her absence, but by spring we had a new summer home.

During the depression years and the war years that followed, our family spent every summer and some Christmases in La Jolla. The house had been designed by Mother who was a skilled artist, and it became the pride of my father's life. He loved La Jolla. During the summers, he spent every morning working, but then joined us all in playing golf, going to the beach club and the races at Del Mar where his scientific betting methods were put to the test, and in the evenings, attending the local movie. The movie changed its program four times a week, and I don't think we missed more than one or two programs a summer. My father loved the Andy Hardy movies as much as I did, and he puzzled through the many mystery stories which were common movie fare in those days. He enjoyed his relaxation and non-intellectual pursuits in the summer. But, as in everything else, he worked hard at it. His golf score was crucial to him, and even the movies had to be seen from beginning to end so the plot could be studied. He was always irritated if we arrived late, and then insisted we stay for the second show to see the entire film. In discussing the plot later, it seemed he really had trouble understanding the tale when not seen from the beginning. Maybe he simply didn't care for that kind of complexity when he was relaxing.

Despite the fact there were no overt displays of affection in my home, I know my father was extremely attached to my mother. An incident which became a family joke shows this quality. When we entered World War II, my mother had not yet taken out citizenship papers. All enemy aliens were asked to register. One evening at dinner, mother said to him, "Feri, today I registered as an enemy alien." He interrupted her with, "That's terrible. They will put you in a concentration camp, and that will ruin me." We all laughed, blurting out, "Ruin who?" The problem was solved when my father phoned some officials in the State Department he knew, and mother had her papers within a matter of weeks.

My father had another side to his character. He was extremely proud of his wife's accomplishments. She became a noted artist and when she had a one-man show in New York, my father delightedly escorted her to the opening, introduced himself as, "I'm the artist's husband." It was a wonderful experience for them both.

Summers in La Jolla revealed yet another side to his character. In the 1930s in the United States, psychoanalysis was not terribly well-known or understood by those who came from old, Yankee wealthy backgrounds. During the summer we would be invited to various social functions in which this group of people were included. These were not like our common acquaintances in Chicago where most of our friends were in the intellectual circle. At parties my father would be surrounded by many "ladies" who, when they learned he was a physician, engaged him in conversations about their blood pressure, migraine headaches, and other symptoms. Instead of being somewhat circumspect about his ideas on these subjects, he used to respond by saying, "It seems to me that you may be suffering from some repressed rage, or repressed sexuality." He had a great deal of charm, so this bull-in-the-china-shop approach was not devastating, even though it embarrassed me and caused my mother some concern.

THE LAST YEARS

In 1956, my father retired from the Institute with regret, and then pushed on West once more in his life. He and mother moved to California. They built a house in Palm Springs where she spent most of her time, and he took on a part-time assignment as head of the Department of Psychiatry at Mount Sinai Hospital in Los Angeles.

It was awkward for him to be head of the department of Mount Sinai's new psychiatric unit without a valid medical license. But, as in many other things, he could do it. Even though he theoretically worked at Mount Sinai only Monday through Thursday and then went to Palm Springs, his schedule was as busy as ever. Retirement was simply not an option for him. His time was occupied by administrative demands, the fascination of conducting major research in the area of psychosomatic medicine, building a private practice, and writing two more books. In the summers, he would attend some international psychoanalytic meetings with his friends from New York, Chicago, and elsewhere. Many times he told me about the adventures he had on his European vacations traveling with May Romm, Sandor Rado, and Marie Bonaparte. I was convinced after listening to them that they had eaten in every fabulous restaurant in every major city in Europe.

But life in Los Angeles was not an unmitigated blessing. He missed Chicago, and he was alone. Mother lived in Palm Springs, saying she had retired from accompanying him to various psychoanalytic social gatherings. Many evenings during the Los Angeles part of the week, I would get a phone call from him, ''Come out to dinner with me.'' If I responded that I was busy, he said, ''Cancel your plans, I can take you to a better place.'' One thing my father hated was to eat alone.

After I left Chicago at the end of my analysis—an analysis which my father remarked certainly did not qualify for following his precepts of brief psychotherapy—I returned to graduate school to pursue my doctorate in sociology. When I decided to follow this plan, I inquired about the local graduate schools. The reason I chose to go to the University of Southern California instead of UCLA was the fact that no one on the faculty of the former recognized me as Franz Alexander's daughter. After three years of graduate school, having established myself with a 4.0 average, I couldn't stand the solitariness of my new-found identity. Now I wanted the connection. One day, I mentioned to one of my professors, Jim Peterson, that my father was Franz Alexander. Immediately he said, ''Oh, do you think he would come over to talk to our students in the Family and Marriage Counseling program.'' I called my father, and asked him. My father was a bit reluctant to take on this assignment. He said, ''But I don't know anything about marriage counseling.'' I assured him that lack would not be noticed. All they wanted to hear was what he had to say about any aspect of psychotherapy he wished to discuss. Much to my surprise, my father wasn't comfortable just to go and say anything that came to mind. Instead, he spent several hours preparing his remarks. I was very proud that night when Jim Peterson asked if I would introduce my father to the audience. Needless to say, he gave a brilliant lecture. The result was that once again people came up and asked, "What's it like to be the daughter of a famous father?" But now such a question no longer raised my anger and insecurity, I was kind of delighted by the whole thing.

During my graduate school training, I received a Ford Foundation grant to study the interaction of delinquent girls with their probation officers. During this year I met Jack Levine, an assistant director in the Los Angeles County Probation Department. I was a bit unaware that Jack was pursuing me with matrimonial intentions since my focus of attention was in my work. However, as time went on I fell in love. My family met Jack. My father was pleased with him but mother didn't like him. She pointed to the fact he had thick ankles which, in her mind, showed a "lack of breeding." I replied that Jack wasn't a racehorse. After knowing each other about a year, we decided to get married.

I asked Jack if he would mind speaking to my father about our marriage plans. Despite the fact my father was on the forefront of psychoanalytic thought long before it was fashionable, he was a Victorian traditionalist when it came to his family. Jack and my father set up an appointment. He quizzed Jack about his background, his career, and what his plans for the future were. In the early 1960s, I was being treated like some heroine out of a Bronte novel. Obviously, Jack received my father's blessings. It was, however, a major disappointment to me that my father's lack of courage took this moment to erupt. Mother insisted that under no circumstances would she go to my wedding: "Weddings and funerals are just the same, and I don't want to go to your funeral." She forbade my father to attend as well. My father apologized to us saying, "You know how your mother is, and I have to live with her." I asked an old colleague of his who had gone from Chicago to Los Angeles with him, to give me away at the wedding. Dr. George Mohr was a good stand-in for my father. After we were married, mother finally relented and treated Jack cordially. My father was a frequent guest in our home.

A week before my father died, I had dinner with him. No one knew he was sick, nor did he. That evening he told me with great pride that the Franz Alexander chair had been established at the

University of Southern California medical school. He went on to explain that all of his life he really wanted to be an academic, just as his father had been. Now that life-long ambition was about to be achieved. We had a good time that night as I told him I too was a faculty member at the same University, I had been appointed a lecturer in the Sociology Department. My father died when he had just achieved one of his longings, and when he still looked forward to conquering new worlds.

Even now, some twenty years after his death, Alexander remains a live figure. One of his books, originally published in 1936, has stood the test of time; it has recently been republished—*The Medical Value of Psychoanalysis*. Two years ago I received a call from Judd Marmor, MD, former president of the American Psychiatric Association and the man appointed to the University of Southern California Alexander chair shortly after my father died. He asked if I would be willing to receive the Cedars-Sinai Medical Center Pioneers of Medicine Award in my father's name. Of course I said yes. It was a thrill to get on the platform before an audience of more than 300 physicians, few of whom were psychiatrists, and thank them for the award. I remarked that not many of us are remembered by others shortly after we retire but I was proud to know my father was remembered even twenty years after his death. I think my husband, Jack, and my son, Alex, were proud too.

It wasn't always easy to live with the man Helen Ross, administrator of the Institute for Psychoanalysis in Chicago, characterized as the "playboy of the Western World." I also think I must agree with Therese Benedek, MD, who accurately described my father in a memorial service held for him in Chicago. She said,

> I have talked about Alexander today as if I were justified in saying that I knew him. In reality, one of his amazing characteristics was an ego structure that enabled him to separate (or even isolate) the "public" from the "private" person in a higher than usual degree. For this reason, probably nobody knew the vulnerabilities of the man. This made him appear strong, almost invincible, and thus an irritating target for counter-attack.

I can also say, perhaps I never knew him, but I do know that he touched the lives of those in his family, and those with whom he worked and taught. The roll call of the people who can personally say, "He Lived," is long and illustrious; it includes William Menninger, Karl Menninger, Helen V. McLean, Helen Ross, Leon Saul, Milton Miller, Thomas French, George Pollock, Hedda Bolgar, George Mohr, Albrecht Meyer, Fritz von Mollenhoff, Heinz Kohut, Therese Benedek, Elizabeth Tower, Edward Eisler, Sandor Rado, Gregory Zilborg, and many others.

About King Laius and Oedipus: Reminiscences from a Childhood Under the Spell of Freud

Ernst Federn

There are but a few sons of psychoanalysts who followed their fathers in the choice of their profession and became psychoanalysts.[1] Among daughters we find more who did so. As to myself, I took quite a detour before I became a successor to my father's (Paul Federn, MD) work. In fact he bequeathed it to me before he took his own life to avoid the agonies of dying from cancer. For those readers who do not know about this distinguished follower of Freud, a few remarks shall serve as an orientation.

Paul Federn (1871-1950) became in 1903 the fifth member of the so-called Psychological Wednesday Society which was formed around Freud in 1902.[2] He was already a well-known physician, the son of the eminent Salomon Federn, one of Vienna's most distinguished family doctors. In 1914 my father was invited to lecture and practice in the USA where he had some influence on the beginning of psychoanalysis, by analysing Dr. Clarence Oberndorf and Dr. S. E. Jelliffe.[3] When Freud fell ill with cancer of the jaw in 1923 he appointed Federn as personal deputy in all his professional affairs and the Vienna Psychoanalytic Society elected him acting vice-president until its factual dissolution in 1938.[4] In this double position Federn played a role in psychoanalysis that must be considered equal to that of Abraham, Ferenzi, Rank, Jones and second only, as concerned closeness with Freud, to Anna Freud.

In spite of Federn's never wavering loyalty to Freud he developed his own ideas and theories which, although based on Freud's work, went into different directions. The most important were a concept of the ego leading to a new method of treating mental illness and ideas about applying psychoanalysis to social problems, which went beyond Freud's own initial thoughts. This is of very special importance because Federn was, and through his work remains, the living proof against the never dying opinion that Freud did not tolerate any other ideas and theories than his own. In present terminology it may be said that Federn expressed more than fifty years ago in Freudian terminology what has become the psychology of the Self. Federn's historical role does not need to be elaborated further here since this was done by Dr. Edoardo Weiss, myself and others.

Paul Federn has called himself modestly "the non-commissioned officer in the psychoanalytic army." He was in fact, however, a man of great influence on the psychoanalytic world, not only in Vienna. His suicide was reported by all news agencies but did not reach the obituary column of *The New York Times*, with the consequences that it took some time until his name appeared again in public. This was also due to the attitude of the New York Psychoanalytic Society which considered Federn as a "devisionist" and not as a true Freudian analyst. This has some bearing on the following discourse because in order to establish Federn's true role in the history of Freudian psychoanalysis, a task fell on me to which I have been devoting the rest of my life.

Being a son of such a powerful and important person could be generally regarded as at least very difficult. Subjectively speaking it was not. Consciously I was always very attached to my father and it is reported that this was so from early infancy. This is not surprising because in spite of a rather awesome look, a big black, later greying beard, piercing eyes under big eyebrows, a thundering voice and a well built body, he was the kindest man, fond of children of all ages, in whom he never could find any fault even if they behaved like devils. He loved all mankind and walking through the streets of Vienna wearing a broad black hat, he engaged the people on the streets in conversation just from a curiosity to meet them. This brought him the sobriquet "Harun al Raschid," the legendary caliph of Bagdad. In fact, a photo from his youth showed him in the costume of an Arabian sheik. His good looks and the above-mentioned qualities make it easily understandable that one of his patients, Wilma Bauer, ailing since her childhood from rheumatic fever, decided at the early age of eleven to marry him. They became, indeed, husband and wife in 1905 and contrary to what Wilhelm Reich claimed[5] I remember them only as deeply, even romantically in love until the end of their lives, which was painful for both due to the severe illness from which they had to suffer.

In fact I had much more difficulty with my mother than my

father. She dominated him as she dominated everyone who wanted to come close. Since she was a gifted and charming woman who wrote poetry and numerous plays, many did want to be close. She was actively engaged in the psychoanalytic movement and even read a paper on the psychoanalysis of serving maids before the psychoanalytic society on November 14, 1917.[6] Freud held my mother and her writings in great esteem which is attested to by several letters to her. She read all my father's papers before he published them. The relationship was once described by Harmut Meng, the eldest son of Heinrich Meng,[7] after several weeks of staying with our family. Asked about his impressions he replied: ''Mrs. Federn is Mussolini and Dr. Federn is King Victor Emanuel.'' At those times it was general knowledge that the latter was just a puppet under the reign of the dictator. After that my mother was called Mussolina, which she bore with a certain amount of satisfaction. Another eminent psychoanalyst, Dr. Istvan Hollos[8] said on another occasion that no one would ever dare to contradict Mrs. Federn. The issue was a second helping from a delicious dish and Hollos said: ''No one would ever dare contradict you, Mrs. Federn except one person.'' To the irate response of my mother, ''Who ever could that be?'' Dr. Hollos replied, ''Your son Ernst.''

That brings me to the topic of this paper which is the inverted Oedipus which I discovered through my analysis with Herman Nunberg who, against every classical rule, was also a close friend of both my parents. My detractors will immediately consider this a sufficient reason why I never became a member of the International Psychoanalytic Association. Nevertheless, I have great gratitude and admiration for the way Dr. Nunberg conducted my analysis. Since then I know that I fought my mother and loved my father, which did not exclude a great attachment to my mother as a child. But this did not keep me from defending my father against the onslaught of her feminine dominance which, for myself, I never would tolerate. Indeed, in my profession as a social worker where women traditionally play a dominant role, I succeeded in my work reasonably well and was on the best terms with some of the prominent members of this particular female profession.

My getting along with most people of both sexes is however not the result of my analysis because it was my personal quality from earliest years. I would say that my easy familiarity with members of all levels of society from whatever nation and culture is my most striking personal quality. Perhaps it has its roots in the facts that I was born several days later than due to natural law and drank so much from my mother's breasts that our nurse exclaimed, "I just hope he can bear that much." I did and food remained for me a very important part of life, just as talking has. I was thus created a typical oral narcissistic character and if I would ever have slipped into any form of pathology I probably would have become some sort of character-disorder.

A possible turn into delinquency during my adolescence was however prevented through a close friend of my parents, Therese Schlesinger.[9] She was impressed by my premature political interests. At the age of six I developed a concept of free trade that impressed her so much that she wrote a paper about political thinking among children. She decided to train me to become a leader of the Austrian Socialdemocratic Party for which my mother never forgave her when my political activities later sent me for one year to prison and seven years to the concentration camps. This acting out of my delinquent traits saved me from less socially acceptable troubles in which I might have otherwise landed during the stormy period of adolescence. My Socialist conviction was however no rebellion against my parents as is so often the case in children of the well-to-do. Both my father and mother were ardent Socialists. My mother was called "the red one" not only for her Titian red coloured hair but also for her fervent belief in equality for all people. My father was also in his heart a rebel. I remember him reciting a poem by the famous revolutionary German knight, Ulrich von Hutten: "Big fires from small sparks do come, let us bend the world or break it" (Grob Feuer von schmalen Funken stammt, labt uns biegen oder brechen).[10] My political ideas were thus not rebellion but obedience which I believe was one of the reasons that I survived even the greatest dangers to life and limb and have basically not changed my ideas even today at my old age.

That means I was not really a "murderer" of my father but a good son. At the same time I shall not deny the forcefulness of my oedipal feelings. Thus I have learned the importance of ambivalence which serves me well in my clinical work. Man is not made of "either-or" but of "as-well-as." At the age of fourteen I was once very fresh to my father which my mother did not tolerate and she demanded some chastising of me from him. Not that she would have minded carrying out this by herself. Punishment would have meant deprivation of pocket money and over this my father decided. "Leave the little Oedipus alone," was his answer. That made me furious and I replied, "All right with the Oedipus—but what with King Laius?" My father became thoughtful, took a few moments before answering and said, "The Laius conflict is but a reversal of the Oedipus, it is nothing special. But it was a good answer anyway."

I thus claim the priority of having discovered the Laius complex. I don't think today that it is only a reversal of the Oedipal conflict, but it is certainly not its equal as even some Freudian analysts claim. Obviously no child can ever have a Laius complex. It can only occur in grown-ups and has but a descriptive, never an explanatory quality. Wishing to kill a son is of course part of many family constellations. I think that its roots lie in narcissistic disturbances, or a lack of maturation on the part of the father. I also believe that the conflict between Laius and Oedipus belongs to the realm of sibling rivalry and general family interactions. It is more an Adlerian than a Freudian term. The Laius complex itself is never unconscious in a psychoanalytic sense but conscious or preconscious with unconscious motivations from the oedipal period.

This brings me to the influence of psychoanalysis and Freud's personality on my up-bringing. It certainly did not prevent my parents from making mistakes in raising their children. We were three. My sister was born about the same time my father treated a schizophrenic paintress in our home, with the assistance of my mother. This case was later published by my father and preceded the work of C. C. Jung. It was a successful treatment and the patient remained a friend of the family. In 1910[11] my brother Walter was born, who became very soon a difficult, oversensitive child. In a note dated 1916 my father wrote, "Observing my son Walter, I am convinced that such a thing as childhood neurosis exists." He was right as we know now, but not about Walter whose severe obsessional symptoms later turned out to be strong defenses against a latent schizophrenia of which he died at the age of fifty-eight. In spite of this affliction he became an eminent scholar of Egyptology and contributed through the translation into German of my father's book, greatly to the development of psychoanalysis. The value of his research work for the editing of the Minutes of the Vienna Psychoanalytic Society cannot be underestimated. Together with Paul Cranefield and Paul Klemperer he wrote a number of papers on the history of medicine.[12] For his work in the interpretation of hieroglyphic texts he was honored by the University of Oregon which devoted a room to his name. It is, from a psychoanalytic point of view, interesting that my brother worked and was creative as long as there was a PAUL important in his life. After the death of Paul Kleperer he lost all his will to live and committed suicide by starvation. My sister Annie must have had a stormy childhood because of the exciting psychoanalytic insights to which her parents were exposed. I can but report she nevertheless celebrated her eightieth birthday as grandmother of five. She was the mother of two successful physicists and of a daughter who also seems to go the way of the Federn family, becoming an anthropologist. Annie herself acquired a doctorate in law and almost a second one in physics and is regarded by her many friends as quite a brilliant woman.

Were we brought up psychoanalytically? Certainly corporal punishment was excluded. Only once I remember my father lost his composure and control as he beat up my brother who almost had pierced my eyes with his long fingernails which he did not allow to be cut. My mother's way of chastising was absolutely un-psycho-analytic: she deprived us children from all attention, saying, "I don't love you any longer." It was devastating and led to quick surrender. But at the age of seventeen I retaliated and did not speak to her for six weeks until she broke down and my supremacy was established. I dare say that the most important result of psychoanal-ysis for our upbringing was the tolerance for our sexuality, including masturbation, at that time a rare attitude. I do not remember ever having the idea sexuality was bad. When I compare myself with my friends I must consider I was more fortunate. Once, when the question of an adenoidectomy came up for me, which I dreaded, my father decided against it.[13] In the course of his life he developed the conviction that parents cannot really educate their children. They can only protect them, which is in fact their obligation. Having been a family physician and internist before he specialized in psychiatry in 1924, he had seen so much family pathology that he was convinced children need at times protection from their own families. To achieve this he developed the concept that an attorney for children should be established who watched over their mental welfare. He wrote a long manuscript about these ideas during the war but found no acceptance. Almost thirty years later Anna Freud published a book with similar ideas.[14]

I shall not conclude my reminiscences without writing something about the social and cultural climate of these times in Vienna. I was born at the beginning of the end of the Austrian-Hungarian Empire in the city which was one of the power centers of the world. My father, who would later in his life develop some of the most advanced ideas about man's mind and how to cure its sufferings, was, as a young man, a dashing officer in the Emperor's cavalry. It is impossible for the present generation to fathom the depth of the upheaval which my generation had to live through. Since my parents belonged to other times and cultures than I, their ideas and values became part of my superego while my ego had to cope with a different social situation. I was brought up with two maids living-in and three others arriving daily for the heavier housework. All this although my father was by no means rich and often short of money. While a car was out of the question, two months vacation in the Alpine region of Austria was required.

My father practiced at home and our lives had to adjust to the patient's hours lest we meet each other. Once my brother, running to get out of a patient's sight, broke through a glass pane in a door, severely cutting himself. There is a definite difference between the life of a child of a physician who practices in an office or hospital and sees physically ill patients and that of a psychoanalyst who practices at home. The latter's activities cannot be explained to a child until he reaches at least pre-adolescence. The work of parents as they see a patient for one hour in a room which has no instruments or tools must remain beyond a child's understanding. Where parents practice outside the home this will matter less. I understood my father, being a physician, was healing sick people, fighting death.

I also understood early that a friend of my father, August Aichhorn, was helping young people in trouble, which sufficiently impressed me to wish for a profession like his. In school, where I had been class president since twelve, I demonstrated that my identification with Aichhorn equaled father through my behavior. Once, I remember, I called a teacher's behavior toward a classmate as "unpedagogical." The ensuing discussion between the teacher and me saved the whole class from a dreaded examination. On another occasion I tried to explain the inappropriate smile of a classmate as a sign of nervousness, not as lack of respect as the teacher thought. My psychological interventions of this and similar kind helped to make me class president for all remaining five years of school.

Thus I may claim to have accepted my father's work and have identified with it at a relatively early age. I did not read Freud's books before my early twenties when I became my father's secretary. In the early thirties a relative prosperity permitted my father to give dinner parties for members of the Psychoanalytic Society. We always had a good cook and the food on these occasions was particularly delicious. For me, psychoanalysis thus has only the most pleasant oral cathexes. Freud's authority I considered without fault, as was that of his daughter Anna, who visited often; psychoanalysis became part of my life. Though I never met Freud in person, his spirit and work was ever present.[15]

In conclusion I don't think that my few remarks have more than biographical significance. If they permit the drawing of any general conclusions I would formulate them as follows: Psychoanalysis as a field of knowledge cannot and should not be presented to children before they have reached adolescence. How to help people by talking to them may however be explained and made acceptable at any age. We owe it to Anna Freud that giving due recognition to the developmental stages of a child is the precondition of reaching his mind in a meaningful way.

How a psychoanalyst behaves as a parent will depend to a great measure not on his or her professional competence but on his or her quality as a person. Psychoanalysis can never be a guarantee for becoming a good parent. It has been described as an impossible profession. Whether this is a fair statement can be disputed. It is certainly very difficult and demanding work. Whether parents who undertake it day in and day out may be able to contain its stress sufficiently to prevent its spilling over in their children's life must be questioned. By identifying these problems some steps may already be taken towards the mental hygiene of the psychoanalyst himself. This was a field of interest that occupied Paul Federn's last years and to which he contributed a few papers on the "Mental Hygiene of the Ego."[16] Much still has to be done in this direction.

NOTES

1. Of those analysts who are listed as members of the Vienna Psychoanalytic Society in October, 1913, in the last available record of membership before World War I only the son of Paul Federn, the author of this paper, has taken up his father's work. Among those who joined the psychoanalytic movement later we find relatively few who did so. The sons of Herman Nunberg, Heinz Hartmann, Ernst Kris and Karl Menninger come to my mind.

2. Nunberg, H. & Federn, E., edts.: *The Minutes of the Vienna Psychoanalytic Society, 1914-18.* Four volumes. International Universities Press, New York, 1962–1965.

3. Burnham, J. C.: *Psychoanalysis and American Medicine: 1894-1918.* International Universities Press, New York, 1967.

4. The Vienna Psychoanalytic Society was never formally *de lege* dissolved.

5. Higgins, M. & C. M. Raphael, edts.: *Reich Speaks of Freud*. FSG, New York, 1969.

6. *Protokolle der Wiener Psychoanalytischen Vereiningung*, Vol. 4, not in the English edition though.

7. The German-Swiss psychoanalyst (1887-1972) who held the first European university chair for Mental Hygiene at Basle.

8. 1872-1957, was second only to S. Ferenszi among Hungarian analysts. He was the first psychoanalyst who became director of a State Hospital (Budapest, 1918).

9. 1872-1940. She was a leader of the Austrian Socialdemocratic Party and one of the first six women to be elected member of Parliament in 1919. She was also the sister of Emma Eckstein, the patient of Freud and Fliess. Their father was a wealthy Viennese industrialist whose family was befriended by the Freud family and a number of famous Austrians, among them the composer Hugo Wolf.

10. At that time psychoanalysts were not yet convinced that a child could become neurotic.

11. Paul Cranefield, MD, Professor at Rockefeller University and historian of medicine, wrote the first biographical study of Josef Breuer. Paul Klemperer, MD, (1887-1964) was professor of pathology at Columbia University and head of the pathology department at Mount Sinai Hospital, New York City. He belonged to the Wednesday Psychological Society where he sided with Adler. After his retirement he turned his interests to the history of medicine. He was also a cousin of Paul Federn.

12. I had an uncle who was a well-known oto-laryngologist who absolutely wanted to have this operation performed. My adenoids still bother me but I think my father did the right thing.

13. Freud, A., Goldberg, J. & Solnit, A. J. (1972). *Before the Best Interests of the Child*. New York: Free Press.

14. Freud had visited my parents of course before his illness, but I was too young to distinguish him from other bearded men.

15. Zur seelischen Hygiene des Ich: *Die Psychohygiene, Grundlage und Ziele*. Bern, Verlag Huber, 1949 ("About the mental hygiene of the ego." In *The Mental Hygiene, Foundation and Goals*). An abstract of the paper appeared in *American Journal of Psychotherapy*, 1949, 290-291.

.

A Letter from
Dr. Alfred Adler's
Granddaughter

Margot Adler

Dear Dr. Strean:

Sorry to take so long to answer your letter. Here are some of my thoughts about growing up as the granddaughter of Dr. Alfred Adler.

My parents were careful not to use psychoanalytic jargon around me nor to pressure me unduly to go into the field.

Growing up in the '50s, I remember "Hush little siblings," a very funny song about parents who read too many theories and tried them out on their kids.

Although I was given little overt pressure, I internalized quite a bit . . . and determined to leave the field well enough alone: A decision I am now beginning to regret and to reconsider.

The only overt psychological jargon from the Adlerian traditions that was pushed upon me was "Social Interest." As an only child I think my parents worried that I might turn out selfish and they emphasized being social, caring and thinking about others.

The oddest thing about being the child and grandchild of psychiatrists is that I, although I'm not in the field, do a lot in my life that's close to the field: do radio shows that many feel are therapeutic, work with psychological and psychic healing and report (as a journalist) on matters psychological.

As I turn forty (last week) I'm reconsidering my career and wondering if it's not too late to become a therapist.

Sincerely,
Margot Adler

Margot Adler, New York.

29

I Look at Life
from Both Sides Now

Elinor Yahm, MA

I look at life from both sides now
From win and lose
And still somehow
Its life's illusions I recall
I really don't know life at all

Joni Mitchell

I am an analyst, the child of an analyst, the wife of an analyst and
a parent. I have been an analysand twice as an adult and once as a
child. I feel that this gives me a rather unique perspective. Yet, the
experience that effected me most was being the child of an analyst
in the 1940s and 50s.

Much of my time in analysis has been spent trying to untangle
what was for me a very damaging and confusing experience. This
process was additionally complicated for me by the fact that my
mother had a second analysis when I was eighteen and my adult
mother was very different from my childhood mother.

My mother's first analysis was in the early 1930s and directly
influenced her parenting style. While I elaborate more later, Kohut
sums of the essence of my experience in *The Restoration of the Self*
on the psychoanalyst's child when he says,

> The pathogenic effect of the parental behavior lay in the fact
> that the parents' participation in their children's life, their
> claim (often correctly made) that they knew more about what
> their children were thinking, wishing, feeling than the children

Elinor Yahm, Monsey, New York.

31

themselves, tended to interfere with the consolidation of the self of these children, with the further result that the children became secretive and walled themselves off from being penetrated by the parental insights.

The fact that I was in analysis myself from age five and a half to nine further confused the issue. I was unable to separate my mother's role and interpretations from the analyst's. This is illustrated by my memory of getting headaches and having to discuss my emotional problems before my mother would give me an aspirin.

On the positive side, when I was old enough to hear about my mother's work with patients I was fascinated. She loved doing treatment and sought out new and challenging professional experiences which she discussed with me. In the course of talking with her, I absorbed a world view that incorporated a theory of the unconscious that made psychological concepts and theories natural and familiar to me. I think that my mother's excitement about her career was part of a positive identification that had much to do with my becoming a therapist.

When I was eighteen, my mother went back for a second analysis. This one was more complete and the mother I knew as an adult was much more flexible, open and interpersonally related. Although I was not consciously aware of it, I think her second analytic experience gave me the sense that psychotherapy could effect personality change and lead to a greater capacity for happiness.

My early childhood experiences were very much influenced by the state of the psychoanalytic field at the time. My mother was analyzed during her graduate work at the New York School of Social Work in 1930 at their recommendation. They felt her anger was interfering with her work. At that time, analysis dealt with oedipal or neurotic material and did not touch on preoedipal or characterological issues. Id was to be replaced by ego. In her case it was mostly superego. She was raised as a Hassidic Jew. It did not take much for her to move from Hassidic Jew to rigid Freudian. The result seemed to be an incomplete analysis that fostered the development of obsessional defenses and left untouched characterological problems including underlying anxiety, depression and narcissism. Moreover, the theory prevalent at the time was not dynamic in an interpersonal sense. People were viewed from the vantage point of biological drive theory. Traumas were seen as determinant, and often permanent. These theoretical premises very much influenced the ways in which my mother viewed and treated me. Moreover, her unanalyzed narcissism made it very important for her to have a perfectly mentally healthy child.

Hence, my mother tried to raise me in a bubble, to protect me from all traumas. Initially, she was fairly successful. When I was eighteen months, however, she was medically hospitalized for a week and I refused to get out of my crib. For a month after that she was not allowed to pick me up. She saw these events as traumatic, and as permanently damaging to me. My not being perfect was a narcissistic wound and she subsequently watched anxiously over my development for signs of further flaws. Normal difficulties, such as shyness, were seen as serious problems and talked about as such. What was mirrored back to me was the image of a defective child. I always felt like something on the irregular rack at Alexander's, slightly flawed.

When I was five and a half, my brother, then two and a half, was sent to a well known child analyst. I asked to go also since I hoped she, who I fantasized as a fairy god mother, would cure me of my shyness. My request was neither questioned nor my fantasies explored. I was just sent. Since my mother's analysis had been "completed," the theory presumed something must be the matter with me.

I was in treatment for about five years and feel the entire experience was disastrous. First of all, the mere experience of seeing a psychiatrist in 1948 meant there was something terribly wrong with me. Secondly my analyst made interpretations like "Did you ever think you had a penis and it was cut off?" which I thought were crazy. Initially I disagreed openly. Then I learned to agree so she would leave me alone, as I learned to produce a problem for my mother so she would give me an aspirin.

I experienced other interpretations, such as that I spilled things because I was angry at my mother, as blaming. That made me feel I was bad and anger itself was bad, despite the fact everyone was very careful never to use the word "bad." They used "steady" and "unsteady" and I got the impression that I was supposed to be without intensity or passion, and that strong feelings themselves were undesirable. I spent the bulk of my sessions for several years discussing my lack of self confidence. Yet, confidence can only be achieved when one has a solid sense of oneself. As we all know, in the analytic process this comes as one slowly internalizes the good self-object relationship. The analyst must mirror admiration and convey acceptance. This did not occur for me.

As a result I came out of the treatment experience feeling more inadequate, more flawed than when I went in. It taught me to dissemble, to be more compliant, to say the right things and to hide. In other words, to be more schizoid. It made me profoundly question my parents' judgment and ability to help. I wondered why they had to go to someone else all the time. They modeled uncertainty and communicated their feelings of inadequacy. This left me feeling unprotected and insecure.

My analyst and my mother both interpreted other people's behavior in ways that did not seem right to me. Yet, I could not discount their opinions as they were the experts. This confusion about the nature of interpersonal reality was one of the more serious byproducts of my child-analyst, analyst-mother combination. It became most obvious to me when I was nine and my mother went into private practice. She treated many children in my school, sometimes even in my class. She was highly respected as a child development expert, yet she was unable to help me make sense of my world. She was constantly interpreting reality in a confusing way, she would tell me that popular kids did not really feel good about themselves, they were just covering up their feelings of inadequacy. I felt I knew better, but could not completely reject her view.

When I look at my career and object choices as a young adult, I can see both my ambivalence and my wish to resolve the difficulties left by my early experiences. I chose to get my MSW but specialized in community organization rather than casework. Then, I married a social worker working in residential treatment, who was in analysis and felt very positive about the analytic process.

In retrospect, I can see how my experience both as an analyst's child and a child in analysis very much marked my professional direction, choice of an analyst and my therapeutic style.

At the point in my life when I began doing direct treatment I also began to consider going into analysis to deal with my emotional difficulties. My identification with the vulnerability of a child in analysis and my memories of my first analytic experience made me cautious both of my choice of an analyst and in my approach to my work. Unlike most people in 1967, I shopped around before choosing an analyst. I looked for an experience as different as possible from my first one. I only considered men. I rejected two people who were distant and I felt were "Freudian," one because he said I was resistant, the other because he wanted to talk about my parents. I was clear that I wanted someone who would talk with me, who would get involved, who would break down my walls. My fears about a repetition of my early experiences and an expression of my feelings of my mother as all powerful and intrusive are reflected in a persistant fantasy I had during this analysis. I kept on feeling my mother would write my analyst to find out what I was saying and that my analyst would respond. Several years later, I found out that an uncle, my mother's brother, also an analyst, had actually written his daughter's analyst to find out why she was not married.

My choice of a second analyst two and a half years later was also a direct attempt to resolve the early experiences. After interviewing a considerable number of people, I chose a woman who, while interpersonally trained, was somewhat distant and definitely not intrusive.

As a new therapist, I began working with children in a residential treatment center that stressed a milieu and team approach. I was obviously trying to repair something for myself yet was using the milieu approach as a safeguard. I was identified with the children and was afraid of the potential negative impact I felt I would have in an individual treatment situation. My bad treatment experience saved me the grandiosity of many new therapists. I identified strongly with the experience of being a helpless dependent patient and, in fact, only began to do individual treatment once I was in analytic training. I did not want to do bad or even irrelevant therapy.

My choice of an analytic institute was also in reaction to my bad childhood analysis which I blamed on the "Freudian approach." I considered only institutes with an interpersonal orientation.

When I look back, I can see how my early experiences directly influenced many of my strengths and difficulties as I tried to develop my own analytic style. For many years, I retained an unconscious image of the patient as a child patient; confused, helpless, dependent and without sufficient ego or experience to evaluate analytic interpretations. Afraid of my own impact, I avoided setting limits, which I felt would be experienced as rejections, and shunned confrontations or interpretations, which I feared might be experienced as judgments or narcissistic wounds. On the positive side, my own efforts to break down my walls have enabled me to struggle tenaciously with patients and remain committed to their efforts to know themselves even when they are most discouraged. As a result, I have been able to work well with many difficult and disconnected patients.

I have definite feelings about the treatment of children. I believe that no matter how it is presented, it is almost impossible to send a child into therapy without the child feeling that there is something the matter with him. Whenever possible, I try to help the parents help the children deal with their difficulties in living. I feel this is much more conducive to the development of a solid sense of self.

My approach to child treatment when it is necessary is best summed up by Dr. Stanley Speigel in his article "Psychoanalytic Intervention with Children" (*Contemporary Psychoanalysis*, Vol. 9, #2, Feb. 1973):

> I strongly believe that therapy with children is often quite clearly indicated, but that the theoretical framework for such treatment should not be the basic psychoanalytic model as generally currently practiced with the adult. For me it is important that in working with children, the emphasis be on the exposition and clarification of feelings, and the rectification of dissociated feelings. However, it is not only extraneous, it is a serious error to try to provide the youngster with any understanding of transference and of the dynamics and etiology of his disorder.
>
> A developmental theory of children should include the natural development of language and understanding. It is incorrect, however, to psychoanalyze children in a way that equips the child with language and insights that are adult and places on him the burden of acting like an adult. Sullivan said that the worst thing that can happen to a child is the expectation of parents that the child develop characteristics that are beyond his level of maturation, at any moment in time. I believe that it is essential that the analyst be thoroughly acquainted with the case history of the child and that he maintain a rigorous and vigilant attitude toward all pertinent data. I do not mean to imply that analysis with children should be reduced to a kind of sloppy, haphazard methodology. I think however, that we must reemphasize, particularly with children, that there is a quality of "soul" or dignity which

must be nurtured and honored and which one must be very careful not to violate.

The central function of psychoanalytic treatment with children as well as adults is to assist, with minimal "tampering" and manipulation, in a natural growth process. It is to enable the healthy part of the person to be the major determinant of the whole person. A natural growth process requires that the stages in development be experienced in proper sequence. This central ingredient of good treatment is nowhere as important as it is in working with young children. To provide insights and verbal understanding beyond that which would be naturally encountered in a healthy growth pattern would be a gross violation of this principle.

It is as parent that I feel the greatest need to integrate my experiences and come to terms with my past. I have struggled with the issue of how to use the knowledge I received in my professional training while not repeating the errors made by my mother. Obviously psychoanalytic training gives one a world view and a way of understanding interpersonal and intrapsychic reality. The task is to discover how to use this knowledge without interfering with the child's developing sense of self.

I can now empathize with my mother. It is hard to see one's child having difficulty without becoming anxious about the long-range consequences. It is tempting to send one's child to a therapist to prevent future problems, to spare them pain and oneself anxiety. I see the parents task much as Dr. Speigel sees the analysts. This is "to assist with minimal 'tampering' and manipulation, in a natural growth process." With my children I take the approach that life is difficult and painful and that a parent's job is to help a child deal with these difficulties. This approach enables the parent to intervene without interfering and making the child feel bad about himself. It communicates the belief that both the parents and child have the strength and ability to cope. I believe this approach fosters the integrated solid sense of self Kohut talks about. It mirrors a positive respect for the child and enables him to internalize an image of parents who also feel good about themselves and their ability to deal with life.

Looking back I see that many of the difficulties I had as a child were a product of the newness of the field and not intrinsic to the nature of analyst as parent. I see my children and those of many of my colleagues growing up spontaneous, creative and happy with a deep understanding of themselves and others and a realistic understanding of the nature of the human condition. Their development seems to have been enhanced, rather than hindered by their parent's analytic understanding.

Confessions of a Freudian's Offspring

Billy Strean

"My father fixes feelings," I told my nursery school class. We had been asked to respond to the question, "What does your daddy do for a living?" Four year-olds have some notion of what a baker, lawyer, and salesman are, but most of these toddlers are not well acquainted with the world of a psychoanalyst. Although any parent's profession will have an effect on his children's development, a shrink's kid is in a unique situation. There are some definite advantages to having a therapist at your dinner table every night. There are also some serious drawbacks to living with an analyst.

Having grown up with a psychoanalyst as a father, I have been fortunate to develop the skills of both a good patient and a good therapist; I have learned to speak openly about my feelings and I have learned to analyze. I have many memories of my father sitting on my bed at night and listening to my problems. I was encouraged to say what I was feeling. I found this quite helpful to let these thoughts out. I also found that my dad usually had a helpful comment or suggestion. I used to go down to my dad's study while he was writing a book or preparing for class and discuss whatever might have been on my mind. The freedom to express myself and communicate about feelings and problems has helped me in dealing with people, especially close friends. In addition, I am more free with my creative thoughts. My sense of humor and ability to communicate have been greatly enhanced by these experiences I had with my dad, the psychoanalyst.

The exposure to the therapist's side of the process developed my analytical skills. In dealing with my own issues and in hearing about cases, I learned a great deal about breaking down a situation and seeing some of the underlying causes and facets. One of my high school buddies wrote in my yearbook that in his lifetime he hoped

Billy Strean was a senior at Grinnell College at the time this article was submitted.

39

to develop some of the qualities that I possessed. Foremost among these was my ability "to analyze people and situations." I, too, have greatly appreciated this in myself in several ways. First, understanding what makes people tick, and realizing the many levels at which people think gave me an advantage in countless situations. I have been more equipped to communicate effectively, to solve my own problems and to be a resource to friends. Second, the skills I gained have carried over to all areas of life. Analyzing literature or trying to unpack the great philosophers has been facilitated by the exposure I had to my father and the methods of his business. My understanding of what motivates people and their behavior has been a tremendous asset in my teaching, counseling and coaching experiences. At this point I do not foresee myself pursuing a career directly related to psychotherapy, but in whatever I choose to engage, I will be superior because of my involvement with the field, namely having one of its practitioners as a parent.

On a Sunday afternoon, when I was about fourteen, having just beaten my dad in a game of ping pong, the two of us took to the basketball court. I was being very provocative, which was probably more difficult for my dad to cope with because he was out of breath. As the game progressed and the situation got worse, my dad lost his temper and heaved the basketball at the ground in my general direction. I calmly looked at him and said, "Just because I have an Oedipus complex, there's no reason for you to act immaturely." He was able to laugh and things went all right, but this scene was very instructive. The reason I was able to say something like that is that I had heard so much about this Oedipus fellow and his complex. I remember one summer at camp I had a girlfriend whose first name, Marjorie, was somewhat similar to my mother's name, Marcia. A big deal was made of it, enough for me to wonder how future girlfriends would be evaluated in terms of likeness to my mother and evidence of my Oedipal conflict. Every kid on the block had a crush on Marcia Brady (of Brady Bunch fame), but I was the only one who wondered what relationship this might have to my murderous impulses. While I was home recently, I noticed that at the mention of some Greek person, my father chimed in with a couple of remarks about Oedipus. I finally began to realize that all this talk about Oedipus is a result of my father's own strong Oedipal conflicts. This is one area in which I feel my dad's occupation had a negative effect on me.

As stated above, there were positive aspects of my dad's

psychoanalytic abilities, but there was a problem with this, too. Although it was great to have a skilled listener who was able to analyze my difficulties, I suffered from premature interpretations. Because my father knew me so well and was confident of his analysis, I was not afforded the luxury of his patients, who might have been able to come to some of their own conclusions. As I got older it bothered me that I might have been reacting to self-fulfilling prophesies rather than what might really be at issue. In this way, I am somewhat resentful of psychoanalysis' role in my development.

With any child-parent relationship there is some ambivalence. My father and I have a close loving relationship, yet there are areas where anger and resentment exist. His role as psychoanalyst vis-à-vis my growing up exemplifies this relationship. Although there are aspects of having had a therapist for a father that I am bothered by, for the most part I am grateful for the experience and I feel I have learned a tremendous amount. While problems exist, both dad and Sigmund will be happy that being a Freudian's offspring has enhanced my ability to love and work.

La Vie avec Maman
(Life with "Maman")

Jane Jennifer Felton

From the day I was born, I have been living with Sigmund Freud and psychoanalysis. Even my obstetrician, who delivered me, was psychoanalytically-oriented and referred by my mother's analyst. With these beginnings you would think it would be easy to write a paper on what it has been like to be the daughter of a psychoanalyst. However, I am blocked.

First, I must think why I, the daughter of a psychoanalyst, would be (if I would be) raised differently from the son/daughter of a person with a different profession. Psychoanalysts, one could say, are usually very astute people with great insight. They are in touch with many kinds of problems and conflicts and can most often solve them better than anyone else. Therefore, wouldn't one then say that they would raise their children without any of the problems that they encounter day in and day out? I can answer this. No, they do not. When I was young I thought that my mother *should* raise me without problems. Now I realize that she, as well as other psychoanalysts, are capable of being wrong, making mistakes, acting like jerks at times, and other "bad things."

Certain things "Maman" (my pet name for her) has done—and ways she has raised me—*do* differentiate her from other mothers. My mother has always seen people for what they are. I have had friends whom I have liked and my mother has not. Often it would turn out that these friends were not so great after all. I can recall some instances where she went so far as to *analyze* my friends.

Seeing people for what they are, and being a bit preoccupied with authenticity, my mother reflects this in the way she acts and dresses. At dinner time, for instance, our family may sometimes read, watch

---

Jane Jennifer Felton was an honors student in Grade Nine at Princeton Day School, Princeton, New Jersey at the time this article was submitted. In addition to playing varsity ice hockey, junior-varsity field hockey, the piano, and riding horses, she likes to keep "Maman" in line as well as in fashion.

T.V., or even talk on the phone. When my mother dresses her foremost concern is comfort. This is *not* to say that she would wear a bathrobe out of the house if she could. However, she has, on occasion, put to use her outdated bellbottom pants.

Furthermore, Mom has always been very informing. She told me how babies were made when I was only three and one-half years old. And no, she did not tell me this in the way most parents tell their children. There were (so I thought) more vocabulary words in this explanation than I had had in my life at that age. Whenever I would say about a pregnant woman "Mommy, is there a baby in that lady's tummy?" My mother would adamantly say, "No. The baby is in the woman's *uterus*." Who had ever heard of a three and one-half year old girl talking about uteri?

Especially in the late 1970s and early 1980s, my mother was not an avid, but a somewhat enthusiastic feminist. She particularly enjoyed correcting various mistaken literary sources when they generalized people as "he." I must say that I did not encourage this usage of the word "he." However, I felt justified in getting annoyed when she would mark in her book "or she" when a "he" came up that was not assigned to a distinct individual.

I will always remember the time in the winter of 1976, when I was five years old, and my parents and I went out in the snow to make a snowman. If you have not yet guessed what we did, I'll tell you. We made a snowlady instead. We gave her a dress. And we even put tennis balls in that dress to add some womanly features in case it wasn't obvious enough already. Our whole family had lots of fun creating this new and unique character.

Something which I cannot explain is why my mother goes on "etiquette binges." This is what I say when she goes from "my mother" to Amy Vanderbilt or Miss Manners. Life with mother goes from "Wear whatever you want" to "You may not wear light colored shoes after Labor Day, Jane! I am really surprised at you."

Analyzing people is what my mother does for a living. I am certain she likes what she does very much because she uses her skills to analyze in her personal and social life also. Sometimes it seems she makes mountains out of molehills, though. That is, she sometimes analyzes *too much*. For example, when I was in nursery school I loved to draw people. I would draw queens, stick people, mothers, anything. However, I did not draw these people with necks. The simple reason, as I have always seen it, is that none of my friends drew necks at that time, so I didn't either. According to my mother, this absence of necks in my drawings indicated some sort of emotional problem. Not that I know what that emotional problem was anymore—my mother doesn't remember either.

With my Mom having always been busy so much of the time, I can remember how I used to feel about it. When I was younger, and many of my friends had mothers who worked in the home, I used to be jealous. My friends' mothers would clean their rooms, make their dinners, drive them places, and be class parents. It was never the fact that my friends had mothers who cleaned and cooked for them, but it seemed like their mothers centered themselves more around their children than my mother did. In sixth grade, I *begged* my mother to become a class parent. My mother was not a bad class parent, but once I saw what it was like having a mother who did this, it was never important to me again.

Especially when I was a young girl, my mother's job always intrigued me. When my mom would go down into her office with a patient, I never knew what they *really* said. My mother had told me she would start a session by saying "What comes to mind?" For some reason I did not believe her. First of all, wouldn't her patients get tired of the same old line every single session? Secondly, this seemed like an awkward way to talk to another person. I thought my mother only *said* she talked in that fashion, but I could never imagine her actually doing it.

Another reason her work intrigued me is because my mother always made a big deal about confidentiality. When I write this, I do not mean that she refused to peep one word about her patients' lives. My mother would mention a patient's situation to my dad, and I, in turn, would listen. When I would jump in to the conversation and ask a question about this person my mother would suddenly give me the third degree about how this was confidential and she couldn't talk about it. Dialogue would go something like this:

Mom (to Dad): Well, his life is a mess. I am concerned about him. His ninety-five year old parents were separated when his mother found out about his father's affair. With who? His brother's girlfriend! And the whole thing was brought into the open when a huge scene was made and—

Jane (me): And what?

Mom: This is confidential, Jane! Now don't tell any of your friends at school about this!

Does she really think my friends would want to know about my mother's work? Of course this is an exaggeration, but excluding the plight of this poor patient, conversations really have gone like this.

I think that being the daughter of a psychoanalyst (some credit must go to my Mom) has given me the ability to be a person with insight into behaviors and emotions of other people. I have been this type of person with friends and family. Once, when I was about eight years old, I listened to a dream my aunt had. I gave her an example of what it could mean. As far as I was concerned, I was just trying to imitate the way my mother thought about the dreams to interpret them. To me, the interpretation did not mean anything, and I did not believe *myself* in the explanation I gave. It was just something to say in order to sound like you knew what you were talking about. My mother and my aunt thought that what I had said showed great insight and superior thinking. I was surprised!

I have gone from being born into Freudian hands, to growing up in them. I have put up with bellbottoms, and I have been put down for drawing people without necks. I have enjoyed the family "snowlady," while I don't enjoy so much my mother's "etiquette binges." I have lived through it all. And I wouldn't have missed it for the world.

Reflections on Being
the Son of a Psychoanalyst

Felix Berenberg

The idea is to set down some impressions and experiences as the son of a psychoanalyst. I am a clinical psychologist, so when my father invited me to write on this issue I began to think about the idea of the "theme within a theme."

I am intrigued with the idea of the "theme within a theme." It has been used as a literary device, from the "play within a play" in Hamlet, to the labyrinthine parables of Jorge Luis Borges in which a dreamer might find himself being dreamed by another dreamer.

This theme is relevant for psychotherapists. At different times we are the doctor and the patient. We seek our own therapy for personal and training reasons from other therapists who themselves have been in therapy. In turn, it is not unlikely that we will be sought out by other therapists (for therapy or supervision) who will conceivably talk about their own patients, some of whom may be therapists. There will be those times when a patient sounds more like a doctor, and vice versa.

This is important to consider. We must ask ourselves whether we might not be inclined to use our patients to repair certain narcissistic injuries that have remained as painful memories from our own experience of therapy or supervision. Might one, for example, attempt to accomplish this punitively through unflinching adherence to orthodoxy, or, on the other hand, savior-like with unexamined, loving acceptance?

In psychotherapy we frequently hear dreams, paradoxes and confusing impressions of how people see themselves in relation to others. This is why this theme is more important for therapists than, say, for surgeons, who also train, are trained by, treat, and are treated by, other surgeons.

When I was a little boy I wanted to be like my father. At first I

Felix Berenberg, **PhD, San** Francisco.

wanted to run away with him to join a pirate's band. Later on, I became interested in the psychological tests he administered. When I was in graduate school and took a course in psychological assessment, my father presented me with his weathered Rorschach cards. My dissertation chairman was also an analyst who happened to have a son who is a clinical psychologist. In his characteristic manner he told me how he had enacted this Rorschach "tradition" with his son. He said to me: "I handed him down the sword!"

I find it amusing that I have chosen to enter a field in which it is appropriate, if not central, to inquire as to why a boy might want to emulate, perhaps even replace, his father. But this is the kind of thing I frequently talk about with my father. Sometimes I think my father may be a father-symbol for me.

What It's Like Having a Shrink for a Mother

Vanessa Celentano

I think having a shrink for a mother has its advantages and its disadvantages. Some of the good things are: she makes pretty good money so she really doesn't have to worry about the price of things (even though she does), and she can help people too. But then there are the bad things. Once, when a patient called on the house phone, I told her my mom was eating. Well, my mom threw a fit! So far this girl knows my mom has a son and a daughter, she eats at night and takes baths. Now the treatment might not work or something, I guess. I don't see what the difference is!

Then there's always my mom reading her psychology and Freud books to my father at night. What a bore! I can hear her telling him how Freud's mind works all the way in my room and in my sleep. Plus, her psychology books take up one third of the house.

All of this doesn't matter though when she can find out what I've done that day from my body language (that's what I've heard shrinks can do). She can also tell which of my friends have problems and which are o.k. for me. It's like having a psychic for a mom. I guess it's not so bad though. I could have had a baseball player or something for a mother!

Vanessa Celentano, Port Jefferson, New York, was fourteen years old at the time this article was submitted.

My Mother
Answers Questions

Jonathan Hefler

My mother has taught me a lot about my inner self and the world around me. I have asked many kinds of questions and she has answered them in a simple manner. Once I asked her a question, "Mother," I said, "What would you do if you could do anything in the world to Hitler?" At first I thought that was a silly question of me to ask. Anyone would want to hurt or kill him. Then she replied, "I would teach him therapy," she said simply. At first I thought she was loony! Then I said, "Therapy! Why therapy? This man killed over six million people! Why therapy?" Then she answered me, "I would teach him therapy because this country says you can not kill another human being in justice before you see whether or not he or she knows the difference between reality and fantasy. That is a therapist's job." Suddenly it occurred to me that, why of course, if he knew the difference between reality and fantasy he might not have done such things as he did. Maybe he had terribly horrible dreams that made him crazy. Or maybe they didn't have therapists in those days. I don't really know though. Personally, I think it's real fun to have a mother of this sort.

Jonathan Hefler, Princeton, New Jersey, was nine years old at the time this article was submitted.

Both My Parents
Are Analysts

Rebecca Yahm

It's not easy for me to write about being a child of two analysts because I still am one, so I can't look back and decide what they did, and didn't do right. Also, I don't know how much of my parents is what they do, and how much is just who they are.

I remember, as a very young child, trying to explain to my friends what it is my parents do. "They help people work out their problems" was the standard response.

Later, I enjoyed the fact that not many people my age could both define, and spell, "psychotherapist."

Being the first child, and an only child for seven years, the world I grew up in consisted of my parents, a dog, a babysitter, and a Montessori school. I got a lot of attention, and I was always treated, and spoken to, as an adult. When a decision was being made my opinions and feelings counted. I've always been treated as a mature person, so much that once my father screamed at me, "Why are you acting like a child!" and then laughed as I reminded him that I *was* a child.

I can't remember a time when dinner-table talk didn't include some mention of my parents' patients. I've always been interested in them and their stories. When I was ten or eleven and asked for a book to read I was handed *I Never Promised You a Rose Garden*. I read it, and was fascinated.

I guess I've grown up with the feeling that people who are in therapy, or analysis, or any other related term, are not necessarily crazy. I've met patients of my parents and not given a second thought to the fact that they were in therapy.

I've always had a sense that there are reasons for the way people

Rebecca Yahm, Monsey, New York, was fourteen years old at the time this article was submitted.

are, and that an event can change a person. I've rarely accepted anything without trying to understand it.

My parents have always discussed things and as a result I tell them almost everything. They know a lot about my friends, from the gossip to the important stuff.

One of the main differences between myself and my friends that I think comes directly from my parents, is that I think about things, and I can talk seriously. I've always spent long periods of time, while lying in bed, just thinking and questioning things that most people take for granted. I am also able to talk about things that are important to me, most of my friends can't get past who has a crush on whom. A few months ago two of my friends wanted me to go to see a movie with them. When I asked my father to drive us one way, he suggested that we just sit around and talk instead. My friends didn't go for that, and although they thought the idea was weird, it was what I would have preferred doing.

As well as questioning others' behavior, I've always questioned my own. When I was about seven, I told my father a dream that had frightened me and he helped me to understand it. I've given my dreams more thought since then.

I know my parents discuss, with each other, many of the things I tell them. There are things I don't tell them because I don't want to be analyzed after I go to sleep. I guess I feel like I lose some of my ''self'' when they discuss things about me that I feel are too personal.

I think that being a child of two analysts has very much shaped who I am. I am able to think about and to understand things and people. I can sit and have a serious discussion. I have a certain basic understanding of people and why they do things. I am different than most people my age, but I like who I am, and who my parents are. My life is more complicated because my parents are analysts, but I think that the effects will essentially make my life richer.

Breast-Fed
on Psychoanalysis

Laurel Endler

My mother is Dr. Evelyn Liegner, *Psychoanalyst*. Of course she is many other things as well, wife, mother, grandmother, educator, but I often felt that her profession was given top priority. Having been "breast-fed" on psychoanalysis has had a most powerful and poignant effect on me. I grew up believing that she could read my mind because she would often tell me what I was thinking, feeling and even contemplating and, what made it worse, was that she was usually right. (Talk about infringing on one's privacy.)

As a young child I believe my stubbornness (or, as I prefer to say now, my strong will) became my only weapon against the many interpretations and "shoulds" that were part of my world. This stubbornness blossomed into full-blown rebelliousness as I became an adolescent with typical angry, negative, self-centered and, of course, self-righteous characteristics. (I must have been hell to live with.) In retrospect I think a combination of "joining" and "silence" would have enabled me to make wiser choices. However the need to prove my parents wrong truly dominated my existence. Throughout this adolescence there was a continuous thread of psychoanalytic theory and practice and while there was a certain lack of emotional privacy in my world there was also a great deal of understanding.

As I matured into young adulthood my mother seemed to become increasingly empathic and circumspect as I was able to tell her the negative and positive effects of her communications. I understand now that my childhood and adolescence corresponded with her "professional" childhood and adolescence. Despite some of the hardships this imposed on both of us, I would say that it was my mother's intuitive practice and understanding in dealing with me

Ms. Endler is a psychotherapist in private practice with a special interest in working with adolescents.

over many years that ultimately helped me develop a powerful intuitive understanding of my own. I believe that this kind of empathic intuition and silent understanding is something that cannot be learned and is bred into one's character development through a special kind of upbringing. So thanks to what may have seemed at the time an overdose of psychoanalysis, I was able to mature into a perceptive, empathic, reflective person with the ability to make healthy choices. Thanks, Mom.

Feel Scared
and Do It Anyway!

Alison Endler
Joshua Endler
Jordan Endler

One of the earliest memories I have of my psychoanalyst grandmother is of her telling me to feel scared and do it anyway. To this day she still says it. She lives in a big house and I used to visit her a lot. I was always scared to go upstairs by myself and that's when she would make that remark. I was only 3 or 4 years old. It's strange because now at 15 that thought always comes to my mind when I feel afraid to do something. She must have been doing something right. Many times these days when I feel embarrassed to do something I just substitute the word scared and that enables me to do it. This is also true of many other feelings that stop me from doing what I want to do. But even though that memory comes back to me, it doesn't always help me to do what I want.

I feel it's hard growing up with a psychotherapist in the family. In my case I had three: my grandmother, mother and father. There are probably pros and cons to the situation. One thing I do know is that they were always looking at something the therapeutic way. It seemed they looked at things differently than my friends' parents.

When people ask me if I want to be a psychotherapist when I'm older I give a quick reply of no. I'd probably be more open to going into the field if I didn't have three in the family. I've become so sick of psychotherapists that I don't want to have anything to do with them. Maybe someday my feelings will change but right now that's how I feel.

Alison Endler was age fifteen, Joshua Endler was age eleven, and Jordan Endler was age eight, at the time this article was submitted.

Joshua Endler

I don't usually agree with my sister but this time I agree with everything she says.

Jordan Endler

I don't usually agree with either my sister or my brother but I feel the same way. Sometimes I think that I will become a psychotherapist anyway.

Mom and Dad
Are Psychoanalysts

Amy Louise Sande-Friedman

I am seven and a half years old. Both of my parents are psychoanalysts. I think my life at home is a lot like many of my friends' lives. But I think my parents understand me better than some of my friends' parents understand them. For example, my Mom helped me once when my friend said she was afraid of my dog, Suki. My friend had never been afraid of Suki before and I didn't understand what had changed. But I *did* know that my feelings were hurt. My Mom explained that my friend was having bad feelings too. My friend did not know what the bad feelings were, so she said something that might hurt me as a way of not being upset herself. After my Mom told me this, I understood my friend better and my feelings weren't hurt so much anymore.

Another time I was upset when I was doing my homework, and I threw my pencil. My Daddy told me that I was angry because I would rather be playing. He was right! And then I was able to finish my homework.

My parents understand that sometimes I need to have secrets and privacy and that's very important to me. Even if I don't go to my parents because something is private, when I do go to them they help me with my feelings. They never tell me that a feeling is bad or I shouldn't have it. I like this. I don't think that my friends' parents help them the same way. I like the way my parents help me.

One thing about my parents makes me very unhappy. They go to work early and sometimes come home late and I miss them. Many of my friends have Daddies who work late but most of their Moms are home more than my Mom. It don't think it's fair and I would like both my Mom and Daddy to be home more.

Amy Louise Sande-Friedman, of New York City, was seven years old at the time this article was submitted.

59

Profound Distrust

I guess the most basic feeling I had as a child of a psychoanalyst mother was one of profound distrust of our relationship. I was never able to or allowed to separate the parent from the shrink. I often found my mother reserved, unemotional, and judgmental, and I remember wondering what my mother had been like before she went into analytic training, and how much of that emotional style she had learned there. She seemed to me to act as a dispassionate, intellectual analyst, rather than as a direct, honest parent during my childhood.

I found two patterns of interactions I think were mostly due to psychoanalytic influences that were particularly difficult for me to deal with. My mother often assumed the role of the omniscient scholar of behavior, and I ended up feeling less like an individual than a lab experiment. I felt she was responding to me not as a person full of feelings that needed honest reactions, but as an object that was demonstrating something she'd read about in a text somewhere. Her responses were very internal—whatever her reactions were, she treated as an academic exercise, a proof of theories for her. She gained "insights" but she did not share them with me.

When she did share her observations with me, it often came across as telling me how I felt. If I disagreed, it was greeted with a casual and immediate dismissal—how could I, a mere child, disagree with such a scholar of behavior? Speaking up and then being ignored left me feeling confused and distrustful. Analysts are supposed to be, first of all, listeners, I thought; but why wasn't I listened to? Was I unworthy? By the time I got to high school and college, she on occasion would tell me I should be in therapy. Since she always brought it up during periods of conflict or disagreement, I ended up feeling that what she was suggesting was not something that I would find helpful, but a weapon. I though it was something that would be used to manipulate me, to bring me in line with her

The writer of this paper asked to remain anonymous.

way of thinking. Needless to say, this made me very suspicious of therapy in general.

I think that being a psychoanalyst was very important to my mother, but that any conflict or dissension in the family was a sign that she was less than competent at her profession. She needed to be in charge and in control all the time, and it seemed to me that she often said whatever would most efficiently accomplish what she wanted, rather than the truth and risk strife. I ended up feeling cheated of honesty, and of the feeling that relationships are based on intimacy and trust, not power.

I think that her being an analyst made our relationship painful and distant. But from the distance I was proud of her for her accomplishment—it was very difficult in her generation to go to medical school and accomplish all that she did. (When I was growing up in Washington, D.C., women MDs were extremely rare.) But also, like children of all kinds of successful parents, it was a double-edged sword—it was overshadowing and intimidating. I had a lot of difficulty establishing my own sense of self. I went off to college thinking that the most important thing about me was that my mother was a psychoanalyst.

Ultimately, I think the worst legacy of my childhood dealing with an analyst-parent was that it left me with the feeling that relationships in general, and therapy, are both manipulative and dishonest, and I've been struggling ever since to overcome a deep distrust of both.

A Psychotherapist's Discussion with Her Daughter

Jessica Barson
Sharyn F. Barson

SFB: What is it like to be a child who has a psychotherapist parent?

JESSICA: Well, I get to hear a lot of things. My ears get used to it. I hear more conversations.

SFB: What are the conversations about?

JESSICA: Oh, about your patients . . . you know, like the one who reads *our* newspaper in his car in the driveway before he comes in.

SFB: What else is it like?

JESSICA: It's good because I get to hide.

SFB: What do you mean?

JESSICA: You know how you say we shouldn't let your patients see us. Well, once daddy and I were in the garage when he was going to drive me to school and a patient came into the driveway. Daddy peaked through the garage window to see what the patient was doing, if he was still in the car or he went into your office.

SFB: How does it feel to hide?

JESSICA: Good! It gives me more practice for when I do mischievous things.

SFB: Is there anything else about being the child of a psychotherapist?

JESSICA: Well, yes. You always ask me what's my opinion on a problem about children and grown-ups and all sorts of people. It feels good because I get to practice being a psychotherapist, if I want to be one when I grow up. Just like people say I'm a small lawyer like

---

Jessica Barson, age seven at the time this article was submitted, talks with her mother, Sharyn F. Barson, Princeton, New Jersey.

Daddy . . . I feel like a small psychotherapist also. Boy! Have I got a lot to say. Oh, and also, mommy can I tell everyone you think you're fat just to embarrass you?

Son of Analyst Leads "Fairly Normal Life"

David Kaley

I have trouble describing my life as the son of an analyst as opposed to the life of someone whose parent is not an analyst because, being the son of an analyst, all of my friends are children of analysts! I think that besides the fact that we take a lot of trips, I lead a fairly normal life.

Once, when I was on a television show called "Child's Play" on which children defined words and adults had to guess the word, I had to define "psychoanalyst." I said, "My mother is one of these. People come to her and tell her their dreams and she helps them feel better. I don't know how she helps them, but she does. I think this is a very important job."

I think some of my mother is beginning to rub off on me. For instance, once when my little cousin Andrew took the pieces of a puzzle that I was working on and put them in a toy truck, I went up to him and engaged him in a game of Cops-and-Robbers in which I searched his truck and took back some of the pieces. I also pretended to be a mechanic and a customs officer, and eventually I got all the pieces back.

In another instance, I saw one of my classmates looking sad during recess. I asked her what the matter was and she told me that one of her friends wouldn't let her play in her game. I gave her my advice, imitating, I thought, my mother.

I don't think that being the son of an analyst has changed my life at all, but I know that I enjoy it.

David Kaley, of New York City, was eleven years old at the time this article was submitted.

65

PART II

The Analyst as Parent

Polly Condit

When I first heard about plans for an issue of this work on the children of analysts, I asked my children what they thought about having an analyst for a mother. My daughter said,

> Well, one thing you always do. Everytime I tell you that one of my friends is being obnoxious, you always say "so and so is that way because she is unhappy at home, or doesn't get along with her parents, or doesn't feel good about herself." You never just think that when my friends are obnoxious, it's because they *are* obnoxious!

I stopped short. She was right. What I had been doing was not only unhelpful for her but was not good analytic technique either! If someone comes into a session angry at you or at anyone else, you listen. Only later, when full expression of the anger has been discharged, do you begin to try to understand together the whys and the wherefores of the anger. And even then, you don't focus on explaining the other person's dynamics—you have to understand your analysand's dynamics first. "What do these feelings mean to the person who is feeling them?" is a question that must be answered.

On reflection, I realized that I was doing several things with my

---

Polly Condit is a psychoanalyst.

67

daughter that were not particularly helpful to her. First, I was certainly being the analyst (though not a very good one). Second, I was trying to understand rather than just react—not necessarily a good procedure when it comes to personal relationships. Third, I was also trying to make my child into the perfect analyst (as I couldn't be), teaching her to be always empathic, understanding and dynamically oriented in her thinking. Fourth, I was denying my own angry feelings that I had during the day and, concomitantly, was denying my daughter's anger as well. Finally, I was not letting her feel her feelings, but instead I was rationalizing, intellectualizing, and interpreting her feelings away.

This incident made me begin to think about the problems of the analyst as parent. Surely we have some special problems to deal with as we raise our children. The relationships between analysts and their children have been shrouded in secrecy. There are almost no articles in the psychoanalytic literature which describe how analysts relate to their children and vice versa. We know little about Freud and his children, especially about Freud as analyst and parent to his daughter, Anna.

I decided to pursue my subject not only in terms of my own experiences but I also decided to talk with colleagues who had children to see if they also had similar or dissimilar reactions to mine. What I found was that everyone I spoke to had, indeed, some very strong feelings about the effect of being both parent and analyst. This paper, then, is an attempt to discuss some of the ideas and feelings that the parent who also happens to be an analyst copes with while doing work in the office and at home.

Therese Benedek, in her extensive writing on the psychodynamics of parenthood refers first to parenthood as a developmental phase.[1] In later writings she amends this to discuss parenthood as a developmental process, ongoing interactions between parent and child that allow reciprocal developmental processes to take place.[2] According to Benedek, each developmental stage of the child activates in the parent conflicts from that same period in his own earlier life. Hence there is continual opportunity for either a pathological result in the parent-child interaction or a chance for the parent to rework old conflicts and come to new resolutions of old issues. For example, toilet training can be a painful struggle for the parent as his own early conflicts around control and autonomy are reactivated by his young child's defiance and lack of cooperation. It can also be very gratifying to feel that you have enabled your child to negotiate through this stage with a minimum of ambivalence, and perhaps worked through some of your own in the process.

The parent's relationship with his child is a complex combination of projections, identifications, and empathic responses. The mother, for instance, identifies with her baby not only as he really is, but as she was as a baby with her mother. She also identifies with her mother caring for herself, and also with some aspects of her father. Her baby may be experienced as a younger sibling from her childhood, and therefore she might then be her mother as she was with that sibling. The possibilities for identifications are endless, including all the important people in the parents' early years.

The child, as recipient of the parents' object related and narcissistic libido, contains the parents' hopes, dreams, and also fears of what the parent once was, is now, and would like to be. As the child goes through each stage of his life, whether nursing at the breast, going off to school for the first time, or feeling the pain of an adolescent love affair, the parents must go through another experience where their memories and feelings, conscious and unconscious are stirred up. New demands are placed on their capacity for empathy as the child both evokes new feelings and also has new and everchanging age appropriate needs which the parent must meet.[3]

The parent must be psychologically ready to move on as the child grows, giving up old gratifications and finding new ones as his child goes from babyhood to adulthood. Added to all this is the fact that most parents have more than one child and are therefore dealing with their own intrapsychic issues on several levels at the same time. Small wonder that parents are so often overwhelmed and confused by their children.

As I think about the vissicitudes of parenthood, I become aware of the many parallels between being a parent and being an analyst. Just as parents are brought face to face with their conflicts by living with and through their children's developmental stages, so too do analysts have to confront their early conflicts as they work with their patients. The memories and fantasies stimulated in the analyst by the analysand's free associations, the countertransferences, and the empathic responses which are called forth by the analysand, are similar to the psychic activity which goes on in the parent with his child.

The analyst, too, has an opportunity to rework old conflicts, albeit in a more disciplined and purposeful manner, as required by supervision and personal psychoanalysis. Personal analysis, the cornerstone of psychoanalytic training, has that importance because through analysis one is afforded the most effective and complete opportunity to work through neurotic and characterological problems. Also because the work of being an analyst is known to reactivate personal conflicts, analysis concurrent with training is considered essential if one is to be as unencumbered as possible by problems which will interfere with the progress of the patient.

Thus both parent and analyst are involved in intense, demanding relationships which force them to face many aspects of themselves which may be conflictful or painful. And both have the opportunity to "redo" their own early relationships and experiences by being intimately involved in the growth and development of another human being. We know that one reason people have children is to try to resolve their own painful childhoods by giving their children what they didn't have themselves when they grew up. Therapists often become aware that one reason they chose psychotherapy as a profession was to redo through their own work the painful conflicts from their own childhoods. Therapists, as children, have often enacted the role of "therapist" or rescuer in their own families. Becoming a therapist allows one to fulfill that role in a way that was never actually possible when a child.

Considering the complexities of being a parent and of being an analyst, it seems likely that a person who is engaged in both careers might well feel some particular strains, and experience some special conflicts. I asked some of my colleagues two questions about their roles as parent and analyst. (1) How does being a parent affect your work? (2) How does your work affect your parenting? Although the N in my study was approximately twelve people, their responses nevertheless are illuminating.

Everyone I talked with felt that becoming a parent had affected their work in various ways. Most of my respondents had been engaged in clinical work before they had children, and had been in psychoanalytic training and analysis as well. Thus it is difficult to make sharp distinctions between the effects of becoming a parent, being in analysis, or being in training. All agreed that their own personal analysis had the greatest impact on their ability to parent, and on the growth of their work. One colleague described her feeling that being a parent and an analyst created a dynamically flowing triangle between herself, her analysis, and her children. She felt that her analysis helped her to understand her child and her work, and her child helped her work and her analysis.

Several who had been child therapists moved away from that

work and focussed more on adults after their own children were born. One cited guilt at taking time away from his own children to be with other children. Another said she felt less libidinally invested in her work with children when she had her own, and also felt that to work with children and then come home to her own was too emotionally taxing.

Becoming a parent changed perceptions of the parent-child relationship according to everyone I spoke to. I have sometimes called parenthood a great "humbling process." I remember the things I said I would never do as a parent before I had children of my own. I remember my not so subtle critical thoughts as I watched other parents in action. Now, although I may still be critical, I think I am more aware of the difficulties the parent may be facing. My identification with the parent has increased. A number of people I talked with described how this increased awareness of and identification with the parent has changed their work. Adjectives such as "castrating," "seductive," "intrusive," or "clinging" are not so glibly used to describe parents. Criticisms of parents, often couched in psychodynamic evaluations are now tempered with more attention to the parent-child interaction and especially what the child's behavior might be inducing in the parent. (Much as an analysand can induce feelings in the analyst.) Several analysts spoke of feeling increased empathy for patients who were parents themselves. Appreciating the importance of genetic endowment, the trials of certain developmental phases, and the anxiety that can be caused by childhood illness were a few of the particular issues mentioned.

A particularly interesting issue was raised as my colleagues described feeling, after becoming parents, both increased or decreased capacity to deal with extremely demanding and dependent patients. One analyst said that she felt she was more able to set appropriate limits so that her personal life was not intruded upon as she had previously felt often happened. Consciously she felt that she had to do this so that she would have the energy to devote to her children when she was not working. But she felt that unconsciously certain symbiotic needs which had been met through her work were now being satisfied by her children. Consequently, because her boundaries were clearer while working, she felt her work improved, specifically her capacity for empathic and ego enhancing responses to patients' demands. Others, however, felt that they had less tolerance or energy for infantile or demanding behavior in their analysands. All of my colleagues described sometimes intense emotional pulls between analysands and children, and were aware that sometimes they were more responsive to one than the other. Everyone described the feeling, shared by all working parents, of coming home to demanding children after a "hard day at the office." But the analytic office is different from most other offices—it involves working with people who may be making very similarly intense demands for your libidinal energy as your children are. As one person put it, "I sometimes feel I'm getting it from both ends."

This leads us into the other question with which I pursued my colleagues. How does your work affect your parenting? This question seemed to inspire intense feeling in everyone. It appears that the emotional pulls I referred to above are experienced more intensely with one's children. In discussing their parenting, the analysts were more self-critical and felt more conflict than in their work. Perhaps this self-criticism is more intense around parenting because of the need we all have, analyst or not, to have children who can be the idealized narcissistic extensions of ourselves. As analysts, we might put particular emphasis on certain areas of accomplishment. Everyone I talked with was very concerned about the emotional health of their children. Knowing that it is impossible to grow up human without emotional conflicts and problems, there was still a powerful wish for this to be so. In view of the focus of our work, this might not be surprising.

I found something else, however, that I would speculate is a result of what I will call here the "analyst's superego." Analysts can be and often are extremely critical of their colleagues and of themselves in their work, and, I found in my interviews, they are also critical of their own parenting. This critical superego is often projected outward, and a number of analysts I spoke to were very concerned with how others viewed their children. Again I think we see this in many parents but the analysts' focus had a particular slant to it. Several described in vivid terms how excruciating it was for them when their children were misbehaving in front of other people. They all felt that they were being watched and secretly criticized for their inability to control their children. They imagined a rather gleeful response on the part of the onlooker, who sees that "shrinks" have the same problems that everyone else has. Of course it is true that we do, and it is also true that people who are threatened by psychoanalysis will often search out any imperfections on the part of an analyst to justify condemning the whole field.

However, I wonder if many analysts don't harbor secret fantasies that at least we should be able to produce the perfectly psychologically healthy child. It can be painful to face that this cannot happen.

Many analysts felt that they had a tendency to over-intellectualize and over-interpret with their children, especially when feeling anxious about what the child was presenting to them. One analyst suggested that we might invade our children's psychological privacy by too easily saying "Perhaps you are feeling so and so" when the child has not yet been able to express or perhaps doesn't want to express what he is feeling. At times this might be a relief and a help to the child, but at other times it might be experienced by the child much as a psychotic patient might experience his therapist: as one who can read his mind and control him. All children struggle with fantasies of omnipotent parents who can read their thoughts. Is this a particularly difficult problem for the child whose parent is able to interpret quite accurately what the child is feeling or thinking?

Another issue which was mentioned a number of times was the analyst-parent's awareness that he often overemphasized the emotional component of a problem the child was having. Perhaps, just as many parents tend to view everything as physical in causation, analysts tend to attribute the child's difficulties to emotional causes while overlooking the physical. One parent described how he felt for several years that his child was suffering from mild depression (as he had as a child) when, in fact, she was suffering from an undiagnosed physical condition. He felt he had been negligent in bringing these symptoms to a physician's attention. Another analyst described how difficult it was to accept that her child's problem was physical, not emotional. Her feeling was that if it were emotional, perhaps she could have some control over the situation. This response, I would guess, is different from that of the general population, where emotional problems seem so elusive and out of control.

As a contradiction to all this, there is the response of analysts when faced by the need for their children to be in therapy themselves. Perhaps it is not a contradiction. We all like to feel in control of our children's destinies. As analysts we may think we have a larger measure of control than most parents over our child's psychological destiny. But when that sense of control is eroded and the need to seek outside help for the child's problems becomes apparent, the analysts I spoke to had very ambivalent reactions. It is difficult enough for any parent to put a child into treatment, and certainly no less difficult for an analyst. The expressed intense feelings of guilt, anger, distrust of the child's therapist, and a deep sense of failure. These are feelings common to all parents when a child enters treatment but the analysts were perplexed by their feelings and found them inconsistent with everything they consciously felt or believed. One said she could not trust another therapist with her child. Another described feeling a failure both as a parent and as an analyst, and felt angry that his child would not be the "perfect analyst's child." In discussing how it would feel to have an older child request analysis, an analyst summed up her ambivalence by stating, "On the one hand I would feel I had given a great gift to my child—the gift of being able to use analysis to enhance and enrich her life. On the other hand, I would feel that somehow I had failed—that my child should have no need for analysis." This feeling was echoed by others I talked to, even though all agreed that everyone can benefit from analysis. What secret feelings we invest in our children.

In this short article, I have tried to explore some of the feelings that analysts who are parents might experience. I am certain that we are not so different from other parents but perhaps the interplay between our work and our parenting affects us in ways which are peculiar to our profession. In any case, in this work in which we ask the children of analysts to share with us their experiences, I thought that we should also hear the other side of the story—the analyst's experiences as parent.

NOTES

1. Benedek, Therese. "Parenthood as a Developmental Phase," *Journal of the American Psychoanalytic Ass.*, 7, 389-417, 1959.

2. Benedek, T. "The Family as a Psychologic Field," *Parenthood: Its psychology and psychopathology*, E. James Anthony and T. Benedek, eds. New York: Little, Brown and Co., 1970.

3. Schwartz, Donald. "Psychoanalytic Developmental Perspectives on Parenthood." *Parenthood: A psychodynamic perspective*, R. Cohen, B. Cohler & S. Weissman, eds. New York: The Guilford Press, 1984.

The Children of Psychoanalysts:
An Informal Survey

Richard Friedman

An idea that every psychoanalyst would agree with is that an adult is shaped by his childhood. It should be of interest to analysts, therefore, to see if generalizations can be made about the children of psychoanalysts. This is a report on forty-eight people, twenty-one women and twenty-seven men, ranging in age today from twenty-two to about fifty, who had an analyst parent or parents. The sample was limited to people who were raised in the United States, as the cultural meaning of many careers are markedly different in Europe than they are in this country, and it would be misleading to compare the foreign-raised with American-raised. Many of the people about whom I received information turned out to have had parents who entered psychoanalytic training after the child was already of school age. I left them out of the survey on the grounds that the child's character would already have been formed and my interest was exclusively in patterns that might be discernible among people who were raised since infancy by analysts.

The sample includes a number of sets of siblings. Seven people in the sample had two parents who were psychoanalysts; sixteen had an analyst mother and twenty-five had an analyst father. Fifteen had one or both parents who were psychoanalysts with medical degrees; the analyst parent of the remaining thirty-three was not a medical practitioner. Many of the children surveyed, in addition to their analyst parent, had a parent who was accomplished as successful in another line of work. Of the people in the arts, for example, at least two have a parent with acknowledged achievement in the arts. At least two had a parent who was a non-psychoanalyst MD, and all of the academics had parents who were, whether analyst or not, in some way connected to the academic world. It should also be noted

Richard Friedman, MSW, is a psychoanalyst.

that the sample includes children raised not only in New York City but also suburban New York and several other cities.

Of the two tasks of love and work, this little survey has concentrated only on career. I do not know how many of the children are married, how many have been divorced nor how many children they have. Nor do I know what their spouses' careers are. An investigation of these questions would be worthwhile.

The result of the survey are presented in Chart 1. The material was arranged so that sex of the child could be compared to the sex of the psychoanalyst parent. There is an apparent tendency to identify with the parents of the same sex. The sons of medically qualified psychoanalyst fathers have gone into medicine at a very high rate (and also into the arts at a higher rate than is true for the children of non-medical analysts).

The chart and the idea of a survey lend an aura of scientific validity to this study that is unwarranted. This sample of forty-eight people is random only in the informal sense that these were individuals about whom I could obtain information by asking colleagues. I did interview several analysts and several of the children in some depth, and I believe that this sample is an accurate reflection of tendencies although a more rigorous scientific survey,

[a] Indicated parent is an M.D.	non-M.D. psychoanalyst	non-M.D. mental health worker	psychiatrist	M.D.s other than psychiatrists	dentists	academics	the arts	misc.
daughter – both parents are analysts	/		/				/²	
daughter – mother only	4	2	/	/		/	/	/ unemployed
daughter – father only	/	2			/	/	/ª	/ª housewife
son – both parents are analysts	/		/		/		/ª	
son – mother only			/	2		/		/ diplomat
son – father only			3 (2ª)	9 (5ª)		2	4 (2ª)	

Chart 1

including a larger and better selected sample, might show a slightly different distribution of career choices.

As a group these people are remarkably successful. Although I do not have income figures, most seem to have settled comfortably into the same upper-middle class milieu in which they were raised. There were no reported drug addicts, alcoholics or criminals and only one unemployed person. It is possible that there are numbers of abject failures that people simply are not talking about. However I did not hear even a hint of them.

The absence of certain professions is striking: there are no lawyers, no MBAs or big business types, and only one government employee (a diplomat in a "glamour" type of work—not what one would think of as a typical bureaucrat). There are no engineers, no architects, no pharmacists, no accountants, nor any shop keepers. I do not have ethnic or religious figures but my impression is that the majority of the sample is Jewish. In a survey of economically and ethnically similar parents who are not psychoanalysts, whether the parents be physicians, lawyers, or academics, I believe that the missing professions would be strongly represented, and that the academics and the artists who are so conspicuous among the children of psychoanalysts would be far less obvious.

One of the advantages of an informal survey is that exceptions and distinctions can be made that would ordinarily be obscured in a statistical study. Most of the non-MD, non-psychoanalyst mental health workers among the children of analysts are social workers. Some of these people are reported to be considering psychoanalytic training. Some of the psychiatrists are psychoanalysts and some are not. My informants were not consistent in their reporting; therefore the psychiatrist children are lumped together without distinguishing those who became analysts. Because such a large number of the sample—twenty—are MDs, I thought it would be interesting to separate the psychiatrists from the non-MD mental health workers on the one hand and the non-psychiatrist MDs on the other. A total of eighteen are, one way or another, involved in mental health work and a total of thirty-three are either in the mental or physical health fields—almost three-fourths of all the children surveyed.

The academics are engaged in a wide range of work from elementary school teaching to university professor and research scholar and, in academic disciplines, ranging from English literature to marine biology. At least one person straddles two fields—a successful educator who is now also a successful writer; he is listed here as an academic. Among those listed as working in the arts are three people who make movies, three who work in theatre, one art gallery owner and (with the educator just mentioned) two writers. Of those in the entertainment field there are no actors and one person who started off directing artistically important movies but feels his current work as a producer is now more akin to business than to the arts. The unemployed woman is also in the arts but has been less successful than these other people.

The housewife upon investigation is closer to her peers than her lonely position in the chart would indicate. She is married to a wealthy man and has devoted her considerable energy and intelligence to volunteer work in the arts and at her synagogue. (Several of the children of analysts have reported a much stronger religious sense than their parents had. The housewife has completed a psychoanalysis. Except for those children of analysts who have themselves become analysts and this one housewife, I do not know how many of the sample have undergone psychoanalysis, or for that matter, how many have sought alternative therapies such as EST, although I know of at least two who have been through several alternative therapies.

Although the data is thin, perhaps it will bear some speculation about the group as a whole. The children of psychoanalysts seem to be highly individualistic, emotive, success-oriented and not easily regimented. They seem to be fairly entrepreneurial, choosing professions where solo private practice, free-lance activity, and non-supervised professional activities are the norm, although they seem not to be motivated exclusively by money. While most are in a position to earn a good living, few seem poised to become millionaires.

One of my teachers, the late Warren I. Susman of Rutgers, used to argue that one of the great divides in American culture was between those he called antinomian and those he called arminian after the two most important positions in eighteenth century American Calvinism. I understand these positions as personality types and, based on my own experience as a psychoanalyst, I think some Americans do take a strongly felt position in one of these two camps, and that one finds oneself taking one of these positions based on one's ego ideal. The children of psychoanalysts strike me as overwhelmingly antinomian. The positions can be understood by looking at Melville's great work, *Billy Budd*. When Billy was tried, the ship's officers took an antinomian position in order to free him; they argued that the law surely could not apply in such a special case, and that with any consideration of justice, Billy must not be punished. Captain Vere, no less a lover of Billy than the other officers, took the arminian position that Billy must be sacrificed to the law in order to avoid taking a stance that would threaten the stability of society. Although Captain Vere could see that hanging Billy would not be just, it was legal, and that to set Billy free would be both dereliction of duty and set a socially dangerous precedent. While many children of many types of professions might agree with Captain Vere, it is hard for me to imagine many of these psycho-analysts' children voting to hang Billy. Analysts' children seem, as a group, to have an ego ideal which values human relationships over rules and to define success as something which includes feelings.

Psychotherapy with Children of Psychotherapists

Herbert S. Strean

An occurrence transpiring almost daily in the office of family agencies, mental hygiene clinics, child guidance centers, and private practitioners is the phenomenon of psychotherapists who enact the roles of patients and clients. Despite the fact that, since the inception of the practice of psychotherapy, the notion that "therapists are people, too" has been held to be virtually axiomatic, there is a paucity of published data on what occurs when the psychotherapist and/or members of his family are recipients of professional therapeutic services. The issue of "confidentiality" may certainly be a factor in our lack of literature on the subject; however, we have been trained to edit documents so that the patient's privacy can be insured. The lack of explication and dearth of literature on the participation of professionals in treatment exists within several disciplines, such as in psychoanalysis, psychology, and psychiatry, and even the "didactic" or "training analysis" has received little written systematic exploration despite its ubiquity in psychoanalytic training institutes.

It is reasonable to infer that when case are reported on specified groups, our diagnostic acumen can often be enhanced and our therapeutic armamentarium enriched. With the recent buttressing of our professional knowledge by the social and behavioral sciences, we have become more sensitive to the dominant values of certain subcultures and ethnic groups. Consequently, when therapeutic intervention occurs, the folkways and mores which affect such areas as child rearing and marital relationships have become part of the treatment plan. Perhaps certain aspects of the "therapeutic subculture" may be clarified by examining some of the results of therapy

Herbert S. Strean, DSW, Director, New York Center for Psychoanalytic Training; Editor-in-chief, *Current Issues in Psychoanalytic Practice.*

Reprinted with permission from Psychoanalytic Review, Vol. 56, No. 3, 1969, pp. 377-386.

with therapists. This paper is an attempt to initiate dialogue and eventual research into this neglected and shrouded subject.

During the past decade this writer has been afforded the challenging and interesting opportunity of working with over a dozen youngsters who were offspring of therapists. Because the data which emerged during the study and diagnostic phases were sufficiently similar from case to case and inasmuch as the children's responses to treatment held many features in common, it was felt that certain tentative conclusions could evolve concerning patterns of parent-child relationships among therapists. Our findings could have implications for psychotherapists at large and perhaps for the treatment of similar occupational groups. While the N in our report is small (twelve cases) and the treatment itself all took place at social agencies (child guidance clinics) and private practice in one city, New York, nonetheless, we are of the opinion that our impressions could serve as a starting point from which others may compare and contrast their own experiences.

THE STUDY PHASE

The twelve cases under review represent children of therapists who were analysts, psychologists and social workers with no one subgroup having a disproportional representation. The seven boys and five girls ranged in age from eight years to nineteen with the mean age fourteen. The approach by the parents to the initial intake consultations was almost identical in all cases. The spouse who was the therapist made the first contact over the phone, requesting "a special favor" or "a very personal request" which "could not be discussed over the phone." Frequently, the parent considered an office discussion as undesirable and preferred a luncheon meeting or social visit. In most cases, the parent only knew the therapist superficially but over the phone he was told that he, the therapist, "knew something about children" and that was why he was being consulted. When the therapist's office (agency office or private office) was suggested as the locus for discussion of the "personal request," most parents balked and either wished to continue the discussion further over the phone or stated that the professional office was "inappropriate." When their preference for the place of the discussion was even superficially explored, in a couple of cases the therapist was told "to forget it" or "never mind, then."

Consequently, as these parents became better known to the therapist, it was considered appropriate to see them at the place they wished to be seen, at *their* office, *their* home, or at a restaurant. After a few pleasantries about the weather and the hectic pace of their own professional lives, most of the parents would initiate the discussion as follows: "I have something embarrassing to discuss with you but I know you'll understand because you have children of your own! You see, my son (daughter) needs treatment." The parents then went on, in most cases, to give a jargon or technical description of their youngsters—"he has a lot of repressed hostility and a powerful superego;" "his Oedipal problem has never been resolved and his phobias certainly tell us that;" "his peer relations are impoverished but his object relations towards adults seem less narcissistic." The parent's own relationship to his child was frequently omitted from the report and, when this was explored, the parent would characteristically point out that the child under discussion related very well to him (or her) but "had some difficulty" with the spouse.

In almost all of the cases under consideration, the parents had received some form of treatment themselves (usually from a psychiatrist or a psychoanalyst) and in a few cases were in therapy at the time of their application for help with their child. They "saw no need" in becoming involved in the treatment process inasmuch as the child's "difficulty was internalized." They would welcome occasional "discussions" or "chats."

As the study phase was extended, most parents and children reported that the following cluster of presenting problems were emerging: the youngster, although usually having had a superior record of academic achievement, was now functioning below his potential in school. His usually cheerful facade appeared to be undergoing modification and he was becoming depressed; in two cases there were some suicidal gestures. The youngster's demeanor was described as "irritable," "petulant," "supercilious" and "sarcastic." In most situations he was becoming unapproachable and in virtually every case "he refused to verbalize his feelings" and was "withdrawing from contact more and more." Frequently, the youngster was experiencing somatic difficulties (stomachaches, headaches, backaches) which the parent labeled as "emotional" or "psychological."

The parents recoiled from any personal involvement when they were asked to present a developmental history. However, despite the paucity of material offered, certain themes were developed in almost all of the histories. The children were planned and wanted. Most pregnancies were uneventful and the infant emerged as "lovable," "alert" and very "bright." Parents often stated that they had experienced "deprived" childhoods themselves and tended to be "overprotective." Overprotection indeed manifested itself by meeting most of the child's demands, rarely limiting him, and with little overt aggression displayed by either parent or child. Sibling rivalry was common but rarely "intense"; "separations" from the parents were difficult in several cases but, almost invariably, "worked through."

During the study phase the child usually was reported as being "very resistant" to coming for his intake interview but the parent "could help him come" and almost always did. The youngster always related very politely in his first interviews, pointed out that he was doing poorly in school but often he "didn't care." When prodded, the child confessed that he was moody and depressed but he usually felt that he "could get over it by himself and didn't need help." However, when the therapist asked if "we should forget about the idea of help," the prospective patient invariably stated, "my parents say I must go." On being told in several cases that maybe the therapist could convince the parents that the applicant shouldn't come for help if he didn't want to, the child often became visibly anxious and brought out "real problems that I need help with" or else extolled the therapist for being "understanding and easy to talk with." In no cases did the youngster drop out in the study phase.

DIAGNOSTIC PHASE

The material in the study phase usually induced a diagnostic impression of the parents being genuinely concerned about their children's welfare but not wanting to involve themselves in the treatment plan. Their difficulty in assuming the role set of client was obvious in most cases and in virtually every situation they did not want their own feelings explored. Guilty, embarrassed, and anxious about their own contributions to their child's emotional difficulties, they defended themselves by intellectualization, denial, and by professionalizing their own contacts with the therapist. Conflicted because the therapist might eventually function in *loco parentis*, the majority of parents under examination were impelled to exhibit their own diagnostic prowess and frequently suggested treatment plans for their children to the therapist.

Diagnostically, it appeared that the parents' anxiety and feeling of vulnerability as parents emerged in their need to control the therapy by not having their own pathology exposed. Their insistence upon having the initial consultation regarding their children almost any place other than the therapist's office was recognized as a strong resistance to assuming the patient role vis-à-vis the therapist. It appeared that whatever intrapsychic conflicts they had, the parents did not want them to emerge in their contact with the child's therapist. This attempt to abdicate some psychological responsibility as a parent also appeared in the parents' major defensive maneuver in their relationships with their children—these parents were overly intellectualized in their contacts with their children and tended to control them by "psychoanalytic interpretation." In many ways, then, the parents did not feel free to interact spontaneously with their children and treated them like therapeutic subjects.

The parents' resistance to involvement as clients was mirrored by their children, who also "could get along by themselves." Although asking for help, parents and children "did not need it," thus demonstrating much ambivalence regarding the expression of dependency and conflict about the need for professional assistance. The most obvious feature of the parents under examination was their oversolicitude toward their youngsters, rather extreme indulgence, and the consequent squelching of the child's assertiveness and aggression. It became clear that the child, who was often described as a "friend" or "pal," was so dependent upon his parents that to oppose or disagree with them would result in overpowering guilt. As the youngster moved toward more autonomy and individuality, he experienced his separations as attacks on his parents and therefore had to retreat with guilt and depression. Although he did not want to see the therapist, who inevitably reminded him of his parents from whom he wished to separate and towards whom he wished to aggress, he felt compelled to obey his parents' command to receive help. As with school, towards which the child had much contempt, he attended treatment interviews compulsively and obediently.

The children most often could be clinically diagnosed as either obsessive character disorders or obsessive compulsive neurotics. While having many ego resources, superego pressures and strong id wishes threw them into much conflict as they attempted to assert themselves. Their depressed affect could be interpreted as aggression turned inward and their academic failures could be seen as unconscious aggressive acts which yielded punishment. Hence, their sadomasochistic orientation was intense as was their pervasive ambivalence.

It will be gleaned from the study data that the dearth of material on the parents, particularly material on the story of their own lives and specifically data on their marriage, prevented the therapist from even attempting to make a comprehensive family diagnosis. Material on relationships to the extended family and on other significant interpersonal relationships was also sparse.

THE TREATMENT PHASE

In virtually every case situation, the child was seen on a once-or twice-weekly basis, most frequently coming to his interviews accompanied by no one. Efforts to work with the parents at significant times were usually rejected politely by the latter but they all continued to ''support the idea of the child's treatment,'' seeing that he attended his interviews and always making sure that fees were rapid.

The children initially came to all of their sessions on time and related to the therapist in a polite but distant manner. They frequently discussed their interests in television, books and sports, and the therapist inevitably joined them in these discussions by asking questions and sharing their enthusiasms. These superficial tête-à-têtes lasted only a few weeks and were always followed by complaints about teachers and parents. The hostile remarks towards teachers usually involved themes of excessive demands by the latter, lack of interest by the teachers and too much distance. When these complaints were received neutrally, the children then launched long expressions of anger and vitriolic displays towards their parents.

Parents were frequently labelled ''unfair.'' They didn't provide for a second television set, a second phone, sufficient clothes, or for the child's own car. The parents did not allow the youngster to ''stay up past midnight,'' ''did not give more than $3 a week for an allowance'' and ''were too interested in my school work and friends.'' During this period of bellowing about parents and school, the parents frequently called the therapist to report that the young-ster was appearing less depressed, functioning better in school and appearing less petulant.

Inevitably, the children would want to test the therapist's stance as to whether he "was taking sides," and the fear was that the therapist would be for the parents or against them. This took the form of: "Do you think I'm right about wanting more allowance?"; "Don't you agree that I should have my own car?" or "Why can't you tell my mother that she should be satisfied with my getting Cs in school?" When questions were not answered but were either reflected or interpreted, the youngsters experienced this as a frus-tration and commenced to aggress towards the therapist. "I don't want you to take sides, you're wrong about that, just answer me!" was a typical exhortation. The youngsters became furious at the therapist for not immediately gratifying them and a period of constant badgering of the therapist with contemptuous remarks always fol-lowed for several months, with a concomitant avoidance of conflicts or complaints about parents and teachers.

The youngsters, contrary to the therapist's expectations, did not react with guilt or depression after or during their aggressive displays towards him. Rather, they continued to improve in school, related with more maturity towards their parents and essentially improved their over-all adaptation. When they were asked how come it didn't get them upset to get angry at the therapist, although they often felt guilty toward their parents after hostile outbursts, many of the children responded with sentiments similar to the following: "You see, you are not a goody-goody. As a matter of fact you don't appear kind or nice, so I don't have to worry about treating you nicely!" One youngster reflected, "You only get upset or guilty when you think the adult can't take it or gets hurt. You don't seem to want me to love you."

Many of the children after a year or a year-and-a-half of treatment wished to quit treatment. They *never* said that the therapist had helped them or that they were functioning better but instead the wish frequently took an aggressive and hostile form: "I don't particularly want to talk to *you* every week; I've got better things to do"; "While I must admit that I enjoy ranking you out, it is beginning to get boring"; "You know, you don't give me anything!" At this phase of treatment they didn't "care what my father or mother thinks about my seeing you, I'm quitting!" Frequently, they contended "that paying this agency (or the therapist) money, is a waste.'' One youngster went so far as to say, "I would rather see my parents buy a book for *themselves* or go to the theater than pay you!''

While the youngsters were attempting to separate from the therapist, they occasionally brought in expressions of endorsement from their parents who most frequently stated, ''It's up to you and Dr. Strean to work it out!'' The child usually set the date of termination and kept his own word.

FOLLOW-UP PHASE

In ten of the twelve cases under discussion, the parents stayed in telephone or social communication with the therapist after termination. While the therapist was initially and for some time suspicious of reports of their children's sustained and improved functioning, particularly because so many of the youngsters left in anger, some understanding of the process slowly evolved. The youngsters rarely mentioned their treatment experience to their parents, and when they did, the therapist was usually described as ''a jerk,'' ''a namby-pamby,'' a ''ninny'' or a ''dope.'' None of the children were reported to idealize the therapist or have positive feelings toward him. What appears to have transpired in the treatment is that the therapist became the ''bad'' parent towards whom the child wanted to aggress. Unable to feel or direct hostility to his own parents or teachers, the unlovable therapist was a convenient target. This freed the youngster to function better in school, feel less depressed, and experience less hostility towards his actual parents. The therapist perhaps could have been regarded as that part of the parental introject who was beaten up and eventually killed off! It is quite conceivable that the children's experience with the therapist was subtly conveyed by the children to the parents, so that the latter got the message and moved away from ''a love and be loved relationship'' with their youngsters and limited them with more equanimity. (In two cases we have actual proof of this.)

Since the process described does not sound like a ''cure'' or complete working through or resolution of the child's ambivalence towards his parents, how are we to account for the youngsters' improved and sustained good functioning? Is it not possible to regard these children as relatively nondisturbed youngsters undergoing developmental hurdles in an environment which was not sufficiently supportive? As the youngsters moved toward more autonomy and separation, they experienced the movement as hostile attacks towards their "loving" parents. Unable to sincerely encourage expressions of assertiveness, separation, and autonomy, the parents unwillingly squelched the child's maturational movement and induced guilt and depression. The therapist, less narcissistically involved than the parents, could encourage the child to cathect negatively towards him, and he thus provided an experience which the parents could not. Because the expression of anger was enjoyable to the child, he continued to retain this pleasure by saying in effect, "at least I don't have to love that therapist all the time; it's almost like hating my parents with inpunity."

IMPLICATIONS

This report sheds some light on the parent-child relationship of some therapists. It would appear from our case material that most of these parents could be regarded as responsible, devoted and loving parents who were overpermissive and indulgent. Their inability to cope effectively with their childrens' aggression and assertiveness tended to freeze the youngsters in their interpersonal relationship. Perhaps therapists, out of their own feelings of "deprivation," tend to overgratify their children (and perhaps their patients, too?), which blocks assertive expressions and the growth process.

A therapist is someone the parents do not want to relate with on a close basis, but he is certainly somebody "who is good for the child." He offers the opportunity to help the child cope with his destructive wishes and to take on increasingly more frustration—so important for the growth process. Whether parents who are therapists are essentially different in their roles as parents from other middle-class occupational groups remains to be reported. However, it would seem that the availability of a therapist or similar figure can help certain children of therapists master the difficult developmental hurdles of autonomy and assertiveness.

One of the significant implications emanating from the data is that some patients who leave treatment with an apparently negative transference nevertheless have a good prognosis. Possibly similar to the parents under examination, who overtly championed a love-and-be-loved relationship with their youngsters, many psychotherapists may regard successful psychotherapy as inherently dependent upon a positive transference and counter-transference relationship. It may well be important, however, for some patients to climb the psychosocial ladder successfully by leaving their therapists in anger or with negative feelings. If the therapist is experienced by the patient as part of an unnecessary symbiosis, as he appeared to be in several of the cases under examination, or as an unacceptable fragment of the patient's ego, terminating treatment with some significantly negative feeling toward the therapist may signify the beginning of healthy conflict resolution.